DEAR OLD SCOTIA

By Alan Hart

DEDICATION

This book is for Mary (Sturdy) Kelefant -- mother of the wonderful woman to whom I am married.

Home

Walking down familiar streets
Remembering times gone by
Feelings of friendship and family
Burn bright in memory's eye.

Games we used to play outside
The places we would go
Carefree days of gentle youth
Time seemingly so slow.

As time walks on, we see its mark
New homes, new stores, new faces
"Remember when" a common phrase
About once familiar places.

But through the years, through all the change
Wherever we may roam
One thing remains a constant gift
The feeling that is ***home***.

~Susan G. Westad

LARRY HART BOOK LIST

The Sacandaga Story	$6.50
Steinmetz in Schenectady	$10.00
Schenectady's Golden Era	$19.95
Did I Wake You Up?	$8.00
Tales of Old Schenectady, Vol. 1	$15.00
Tales of Old Schenectady, Vol. 2	$15.00
Schenectady: A Pictorial History	$16.95
Best of Old Dorp, Book One	$16.95
Hospital on the Hill	$10.00
Through the Darkest Hour	$10.00
Schenectady: Facts & Stuff (Booklet)	$1.75
Pictures From the Past	$15.00
This I Remember....Growing Up In Schenectady	$15.00
ALCO Booklet	$3.00

RUTH HART BOOK LIST

Blabbermouth	$10.00

ALAN HART BOOK LIST

Larry Hart, My Dad	$14.00

To order any of the aforementioned books, please include $3 per book for handling.

Mail to:
Old Dorp Books
120 Waters Road
Scotia, New York 12302

Or Call:
(518) 887-5789

"Nothing is wasted
that makes a memory."

— Larry Hart

TABLE OF CONTENTS

PREFACE

Quite simply, this is a book about what it was like to grow up in the wonderful, little upstate New York village of Scotia during the 1950s and 1960s.

My dear father Larry Hart, who died on February 10, 2004, left behind for me at least one specific writing task to accomplish which he himself never quite got around to doing -- to produce a definitive book about life in Scotia during the second half of the 20th century.

Dad wrote 14 books in his illustrious, prolific 83-year lifetime. (He had started a 15th which he never got to finish. You will find the incompleted work at the end of this book.)

Scotia is my hometown and (if you count living nine miles outside of town in West Glenville as still Scotia) the place I have lived for all but a little over a year of my 57 years. Dad, though he included history and memories of Scotia in several of his books, never devoted a whole volume to the village -- even though he loved it as much as his son does.

I am glad Dad left the job to me. I have always enjoyed Scotia (AND Glenville; it's impossible,because of suburban sprawl, to define where one ends and the other begins these days), and I have always been proud to say I come from Scotia.

Let me say to you most emphatically: the happiest time of my life, as I begin this book in 2004, is right now! Whenever I hear people say, "(Such-and-such) was the best time of my life," I cringe. I believe that to say such a thing is an insult to whoever you are with as a spouse or soulmate at the present time, because you're telling that person you aren't as happy now as you once were. Think about it.

Having said that, though, I know I am lucky -- just as anyone who grew up in Scotia in the last half of the 20th century is lucky -- to call the Village of Scotia my hometown. How do I know this? I went to college in Troy (Hudson Valley Community College) and

Albany (now referred to as University at Albany, though it was called Albany State when I went there back when buffaloes roamed the Earth.) At those schools, and also during my enjoyable 35-year career as a sports writer for the Albany *Times Union* newspaper, people I came in contact with often said "Scotia? Where the heck is that?"

I'd be flabbergasted that they didn't know about my hometown. I'd answer, "Scotia is right across the river from Schenectady. Don't you know what a great place it is? The more I see of the rest of the world, the happier I am that I grew up -- and still live -- in Scotia."

I meant it then, and I still do. I was a boy and a teen-ager and young man in Scotia. After serving two months of basic training at Lackland Air Force Base in San Antonio, Tex., in 1968, I came home and lived in Schenectady for about a year and a half. Then I returned to Scotia in 1970 and, finally, Glenville in 1972. I've lived just outside Scotia ever since and have no plans to move.

Why should I?

When I was a kid and teen, I lived with my slightly older sister, Bonnie, and of course with Dad and Mom -- the former Ruth Brooks of Scotia -- in an area a couple of blocks north of a backwater branch of the Mohawk River. It was a bustling, noisy neighborhood ... especially during the months of the school calendar, because our house at 208 Sanders Avenue was directly across from the side door of Mohawk School -- one of the village's elementary schools. It had a massive (it wasn't, but it seemed huge to me at the time) playground where I could always find other kids who were ready to play baseball, swing on swings, get into innocent mischief or just hang out together.

On the corner to our left at Sanders and South Ten Broeck Street was the Riverside Dairy and ice cream store. Ice cream cones were a dime apiece there back then -- 20 cents if you wanted a double scooped cone. Something called a "Brown Cow," which was a large milk shake in a waxed paper cup, was 50 cents and worth every penny.

My sister, now Bonnie Munro of New Scotland, and I both had friends all up and down the street and neighboring streets and avenues. We had a big, grassy backyard at 208 Sanders. We had great parents and equally caring maternal grandparents (Leslie and Cecile Brooks, who lived a few blocks away.) What more could a kid ask for growing up?

And in the unlikely event that there was actually nothing going on in our neighborhood on a particular day, why, heck -- we were only a two-minute walk from Mohawk Avenue, the main artery of Scotia. That's where the fire station, the post office, the movie theater, the bowling alleys, several restaurants, bakeries, delicatessens, grocery stores, Swire's department store and just about anything else could be reached on foot in a matter of minutes. (It was even faster by bike, of course!)

Further down at the end of Mohawk Avenue, just before the Western Gateway Bridge, was beautiful Collins Park and the great, old library (historic Abraham Glen House), the Little League ballpark, Collins Lake, the Mohawk River and -- let's not forget -- Jumpin' Jacks. (Back in the "old" days, in the late 1950s, it was called the Twin Freeze and the Charcoal Pit.)

I am probably wasting your time attempting this tribute to Scotia if you have never been to Jumpin' Jacks and stood in a long, serpentine line that stretches out to Schonowee Avenue to wait your turn to order a couple of cheeseburgers, an order of fries and an order of onion rings. I make pretty darn good hamburgers myself, if I may say so. But when I really want a burger, there is only one place in the world to go for it and that is Jack's.

Are there better places in the world to call your hometown? Undoubtedly. I'm sure I'd have a different perspective on Scotia had I grown up in Honolulu or some warm, wickedly delicious, sunny place in Georgia, Arizona or Florida. After all, I am one who hates winter. I intensely dislike the cold and the snow and the ice and all the work associated with the endless wintry months of upstate New York. We here in Scotia must deal with these rough elements for pretty close to seven months a year, depending on the severity of the winter.

But as I have gotten older and, ahem, more mature, I have faced the reality that I had better start trying to enjoy the winters which I still have left because there may not be that many more of them. Thus, I have begun to savor -- sort of -- the peace, serenity and slower pace that comes with the cold months.

Being retired helps. (I retired on June 1, 2003.)

I love Scotia. Truly. A couple of years ago, to my absolute delight, my Blue Jays baseball team in the Capital District Men's Senior Baseball League (an adult amateur recreation league) played a couple of our games in Collins Park down at the old diamond near the lake. I got the chance to tell my teammates and some opponents about some of the history of the village, and to point out some of its charm. I was very proud to show off my hometown to them. I believe they were very envious. I don't blame them.

Did I enjoy every single minute of growing up in Scotia? No, of course not. One major problem area for me in that regard was high school. I mean, not only did I dislike high school -- which I of course freely admit now was necessary and character-building in a sad and demented way -- but I HATED high school; at least, for the first two-plus years I was there. Sure, I enjoyed seeing my friends (AND girlfriends, when I was fortunate enough to have one of those!)

I loved playing sports, too: baseball (JV as a sophomore and junior, varsity as a senior) and varsity soccer as a senior in 1963. I am proud to say I was the starting goalkeeper on the very first soccer team Scotia High ever had. But except for the interaction with my friends and girlfriends, and except for sports events and practices, each day I pretty much dreaded going to the high school and could not wait until the bell mercifully rang at 2:36 p.m. to release us to go home or to after-school sports games or practices. Yes, of course I realize now what a great opportunity I wasted. I could have made life so much easier if I had only "applied myself," as so many adults strongly suggested to me in those years. What can I tell you? The "common sense" area of my tiny brain didn't activate until I was into my first or second month of 11th grade. Hey ... nobody's perfect.

In the many pages which follow, I will share with you many memories of growing up in Scotia during the 1950s and early 60s. You will hear not only from me, but from others who experienced this era of Scotia's history -- either as a young person or as an adult.

The format for most of this book shall be that I'll start each chapter with some memories of the topic, then turn the chapter over to one or more of the sources I spoke with ... in order that you will hear from some more "voices" of these years.

I hope you will enjoy this sentimental journey.

Oh, one last thing before we get started. Maybe you are curious about the title of this book. If you are from Scotia and attended the high school, you probably already know the answer. The words are parts of two lines from our high school Alma Mater.

Ugh, the Alma Mater! It was one of the things I hated most about that whole high school time of 1960-64. It was bad enough having a "Tartan" for our mascot and nickname. Other schools had tough, cool nicknames like "Vikings," "Warriors," "Spartans" or "Indians." Scotia? We were the Tartans, and we had a goofy looking guy wearing a beany and a skirt as our caricature mascot, for Heaven's sake! (Obviously, our pedantic forefathers did have a good reason for having designated Tartans as our nickname since the name Scotia means "Land of the Scots" in honor of Alexander Lindsey Glen, a native of Scotland who settled here in 1658. Still ... I've never liked it.)

But that Alma Mater. Fooey! I absolutely loathed sitting in the bleachers of the gym during one of the God-awful, last-period-of-the-day pep rallies and having to sit there while the snooty (sorry ... I thought most of them were!) cheerleaders came tip-toeing out on the floor in single file wearing those silly grins and carrying those pom-poms and megaphones to lead the student body in the singing of the Alma Mater. God, what torture.

Remember?

"Come now cheer for dear old Scotia
Let your voices fill the air.
Our hearts beat high with rapture
(Interruption here: We wiseguy boys at this juncture used to sing "Rupture" instead, then giggle like the immature guys we were.)
As we see our colors fair.
In our work as in our pleasure
For our high school we will fight
As we cheer for dear old Scotia
And the crimson and the white."

Gosh, doesn't it make your heart skip a beat? No? Mine either, actually. Never did. I had team spirit for the teams I played on, but very little school spirit. In fact, in my senior year I used to go to our football games and actually hoped the other school would win, because we soccer players had a very big and very real rivalry with the football players. They called us "girls" and we called them "spastics." Nice, huh?

The Alma Mater IS a kind of catchy tune, all the same. Certainly unforgettable. Thus the title of this book.

I thought briefly about calling the book "My Little Town," after the Paul Simon song. But I decided against that title for a couple of reasons: it doesn't say "Scotia" to me, plus Simon's song really is quite sad and regretful, so it doesn't work here. In fact, John Cougar Mellenkamp's peppy song about growing up in a small town would be much more fitting for my purposes here.

But again, "Dear Old Scotia" seems more appropriate. To me, Scotia IS dear. And in simple fact, it IS old. In fact, Scotia is celebrating its 100th birthday as an incorporated village as I work on this volume.

Here's to you, Scotia, my hometown. I love ya!

A.R.H.

PART I

"Pass the Popcorn, Please!"

If, like me, you were a kid in Scotia during the 1950s, then you no doubt spent many a happy, carefree Saturday afternoon inside the Scotia Theater watching the "Kiddies' Saturday Matinee."

Admission was just 25 cents, and for that quarter you got to see (but not always HEAR due to the hundreds of excited, screaming voices) eight or 10 cartoons, a couple of episodes of The Three Stooges and, finally, a full-length feature film. It was usually a western or adventure film, or maybe a science fiction movie thriller or a Disney film. Or a "Lassie" movie.

What a bargain, and what an escape for us kids.

I can still remember, also, the proprietor -- Mr. Val Ritchey -- turning the houselights back on for a few minutes just before the big movie, and coming down to the front row on the right aisle and reading off the numbers of four or five lucky ticket stubs. If your ticket stub numbers matched what Mr. Ritchey had read, why you would yell with delight and you ran down the aisle to the front where he was standing and waiting with a popcorn bag that was full of candy, gum and other prizes. (I remember winning this prize once, and it was a huge thrill for 7 or 8-year-old Alan Hart.)

I vividly recall getting carried away one particular afternoon after my next-door neighbor and buddy Billy Vazal and I had seen the film "Robinson Crusoe" one fateful afternoon at the matinee. What did we do? Billy and I ran home and decided it would be fun to cut down most of that big, old, thick bush that divided our two properties on Sanders Avenue. We made a little "fort" to play in just like Robinson Crusoe's that afternoon. It seemed like a great idea at the time. That "great idea" soon backfired big time, however, because it wasn't very much later when Billy's father and my own dad came home and discovered the mischief their sons had gotten into that day. Yes, that was the last matinee I saw for awhile. Dad

This photograph from the early 1950s, looking east on Mohawk Avenue, shows Scotia Theater on the right with its marquee announcing a double feature of "Desk Set," and "The Wayward Bus." (Photo courtesy of Paul Ritchey.)

Scotia Cinema at 117 Mohawk Avenue, from the front, as it looked in July of 1987. Notice the old watch and clock repair store on the left of the theater. (Larry Hart collection.)

was pretty steamed, because that gaping hole in the bush would be there a long, long time.

Another vivid memory I have of the old Scotia Theater is this: I was walking to services at the First Baptist Church of Scotia, located on Mohawk Avenue, one late-summer Sunday morning with my grandmother Cecile Brooks. I looked up and noticed that the marquee of the theater, which had been closed all summer for renovations, suddenly was announcing in big, bold letters: Re-opening Sept. 11 with "Prince Valiant."

Wow! I was overjoyed, because I was a kid who was really crazy about Prince Valiant. I had the sword (plastic with a fake ruby in the handle), a clean garbage can lid for a shield, and my mother had made me a blue cape to wear. I had already seen the movie in one of the larger theaters in Schenectady, and I absolutely loved it.

My grandmother, noting my glee over the re-opening, observed with a smile, "Well, that's TWO things to look forward to that day, because September 11th is my birthday."

(Note: If you've never seen "Prince Valiant," it stars Robert Wagner as the title character and has a cast that also includes James Mason, Janet Leigh and Sterling Hayden. It really was a pretty cool flick for the early 1950s, although I suppose today's sophisticated kids would consider it pretty campy, and I guess it was. But me? I loved it.)

In the ensuing years while I was growing up, I saw many, many movies there, not just at the matinees but in the evening with my mother, father and sister, or with teen pals. I distinctly remember seeing "From the Earth to the Moon" there one Friday night with junior high buddy Bruce Holmwood, and the movie was a pretty darn good rendition of the Jules Verne classic novel. It starred Joseph Cotten and George Sanders, and the reason I mention it is because I have never seen the film offered anywhere on VHS or DVD. I'd love to get a copy and see it again.

For a time in my later teen years, the theater became known as the Scotia Art Theater and featured a pretty steady diet of foreign films. Once in awhile the theater still offered an American-made

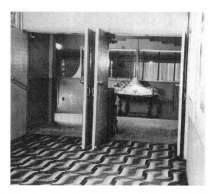

The husband and wife team of Helen Ritchey (top left) and Val Ritchey (bottom right, holding young son Paul) operated the Scotia Theater from 1948 until 1965 when they turned it over to son Paul and their daughter-in-law, Catherine. The scenes inside the theater, taken in the early 1950s, show the interior before renovations were made in 1954 to accomodate Cinemascope movies with a wider screen. (Photos courtesy of Paul Ritchey.)

movie that was considered, you know, kind of "artsy" or special. On just such an occasion as an older teen on a date in the mid-1960s, I saw the lengthy "Doctor Zhivago" one very warm, stuffy summer evening in the crowded balcony of the theater. Yes, the movie is pretty good, I suppose, but for a few years afterward I still cringed whenever I heard that "Lara's Theme" played anywhere. (OK, so it isn't one of my favorite films. You get the idea. The cliche of "chick flick" applies here.)

The theater changed ownership again in the mid-1970s, when I was a young man. I had the distinct pleasure of performing there on its new stage (April 10, 1977) with my then-singing partner, Tim Sawicki, at a "Folk Festival." It was a concert to benefit the American Cancer Society, and the truth is that I organized the show myself to try to raise money for cancer research. (Several people very close to me had just died of cancer.) The new owner, Jerry O'Meara, was very accomodating in helping us get the show off the ground and allowing us the use of the theater that April night. It was a moderate success from a financial standpoint. Truthfully, it would have been a disaster had it not been for the fact that 90 percent of the audience had turned out to see my buddy Tim and one whole other act. It was a talented quintet made up of two boys and three girls from Scotia High. They called themselves "Earthwood," and they were very, very good! (The group was composed of Diane Smolenski, Louise Simoni, Terri Szablewski, Paul Cremo and Brad Littlefield. Boy, could they play and sing -- as could my young buddy, Tim!)

I also had managed to book John Thibodeau, a blues singer/guitarist from Windsor, Ontario. Sawicki and I had met John when we had the honor of performing at the storied Cafe Lena in Saratoga Springs a few months earlier as John's warmup act.

Also performing that evening were the Irish folk duet of Fred LeBrun and Dick Mann, plus David Phillips -- an old college friend from North Greenbush who also was a former singing partner of mine during the folk music era.

A talented group of teen-agers from Scotia High named "Earthwood" entertained at a memorable Folk Festival concert at the Scotia Theater in April of 1977. Front row, from left, are Paul Cremo, Diane Smolenski and Brad Littlefield. Top row, from left, are Terri Szablewski and Louise Simoni. Also appearing that night was a pair of friends named Alan Hart, left, and Tim Sawicki. (Photos courtesy of Joan Szablewski and Tim Sawicki.)

The theater changed hands again in 1981 when it was purchased by current owner, Richard Adams. The name of the theater also was changed at that time to its current "Scotia Cinema."

My wife Mary Carol (Kelefant, Westad) Hart and I truly enjoy going there for films, still. In fact, many times we wait until a movie comes there to see it, because it is such a cozy, homey kind of place to enjoy a movie as opposed to the small, sterile mall theaters. We like to sit down on the right nearest the wall near the front where there are only two seats in a row, because then we know we don't have to keep getting up for people going in and out of the row. One of our favorite nights out these days is to go to the Dragon Garden on Mohawk Avenue for the Chinese food buffet, then walk across the street to take in a movie.

* * *

I spoke at length one wintry afternoon with the husband and wife team of Paul and Catherine Ritchey of Scotia. Paul's father and mother, Val and Helen Ritchey, bought the theater in the summer of 1948. The elder Ritcheys moved to Florida in 1965 and remained the principal owners, doing the paperwork and administration from out of state until they sold it in 1974. But son Paul and daughter-in-law Cathie Ritchey (they married in 1964) ran the theater as Scotia Theater (and then Scotia Art Theater) from 1965 until 1974.

Paul and Catherine Ritchey

They also ran a laundry and dry cleaning business out of the Glen Avenue end of the building.

Paul and Catherine have many, many fond memories of their years in the movie business. Paul, who also worked many years for Sears and also in sales for the *Daily Gazette*, and Catherine, still a member of the management team at Baptist Health,

Nursing and Rehabilitation Center on Route 50, were almost wistful as they talked about their years with the old theater.

"It was built in 1926 by the Farash Theatre Company -- the same company that built the State Theater and Wedgeway (later Erie) Theater in Schenectady," Paul said. "It was known as the Ritz Theater when it opened."

Paul's parents, who hailed from a suburb of Pittsburgh, Pa., moved to Scotia in 1948 to fulfill one of Paul's lifelong dreams.

"Dad was working on Wall Street in New York City. He was working for Sylvania, but he really had the urge to own a movie theater," Paul said. "First, he got a lead on a theater that was for sale in the New Hartford/Utica area. But he really didn't care for that one. He came to Scotia in July of 1948 -- when I was 14 -- and the theater here was for sale. It was owned at the time by the Schine Company. Well, this was the theater he wanted. Dad and Mom bought the theater and his dream had come true."

After awhile, the elder Ritcheys learned that dreams can sometimes turn into a nightmare now and then.

"Things went very well those first couple of years," Paul said. "Tickets were 40 cents for adults and 20 cents for kids, and popcorn was 25 cents a box. We bought a new popcorn maker and the popcorn was delicious. But around 1950 or 1951, Dad had to go get a regular job with GE -- like he'd had with Sylvania -- because the theater business was slowing down. He'd work at the GE in the daytime, come home and run the theater at night and try to get a little sleep before going back to work again in the morning. He had it tough."

Why was the movie business slowing down?

"Everybody was staying home and watching this new thing called television," Catherine Ritchey explained. "Instead of going out, they could stay home and watch Milton Berle on their own screen in their own living room."

Val Ritchey wasn't the only one who found a way to supplement the family income. Helen, Val's wife and Paul's mom, opened a doughnut shop next to the theater. And she showed free

14

movies -- usually some short subjects, cartoons and The Three Stooges -- to patrons who came in during the noon lunch hour to her shop for doughnuts and sandwiches. Anna Ritchey, Helen's daughter and obviously, Paul's sister, played the organ before the free movies. (Anna later went off to Westminster Choir College.)

Soon, though, the Scotia Theater was vibrant again.

"The theater originally seated 500 people when my parents bought it, but in the summer of 1953 they renovated the theater to accomodate a new, big Cinemascope screen," Paul said, referring to the author's earlier mention of the "Prince Valiant" re-opening notice of September 11 of that year. "That renovation brought a lot of people back, plus Dad and Mom tried a lot of gimmicks to bring more people into the theater."

Such as?

"They had those Kiddies' Matinees on Saturday, they had "Dish Night" on Tuesdays when they'd give away dishes, and they had a "Bingo Night" once a week that was very popular. One time, Dad hired a yo-yo man -- an Oriental fellow -- to come in and put on a yo-yo demonstration before the movie. People loved it," Paul Ritchey said.

He added, "You know, Dad and Mom never got rich from the theater, and neither did Cathie and I, but it was fun. When I was a teen-ager I worked there for my father, naturally, before I went off to college at the University of Pittsburgh. One of my jobs was to change the marquee and the posters, and another was to carry out the ashes every morning from the coal furnace before we changed over to oil heat in the mid-1950s."

In 1965, newlyweds Paul and Cathie Ritchey, with the help of about a half-dozen part-time employees, took over the actual operation of the theater. Heidi, the couple's only child, was born in 1966. While Val Ritchey ran the "financial end" of the business from Florida, it was Paul and Cathie who ran the movie house from then on until 1974.

"After I got pregnant, I worked there right up almost until Heidi's birth, and after she was born I took my child with me to work at the ticket booth," Catherine remembers, a knowing smile covering her face. "Then when we converted over to Scotia Art Theater and started showing foriegn films, we added a coffee bar to the lobby, and I used to take care of that. People used to enjoy going in there while they were waiting for the movie, and often afterwards the customers would go in for coffee to discuss the movie they had just seen."

Both Paul and Catherine Ritchey were quick to point out that "Art" theater did not mean "X-rated" or off-color. There was never anything lewd about the movies their theater showed.

"I remember one time people were kind of disappointed, because there was a French movie called 'The Lovers' that was actually banned from American theaters for awhile before we got to show it," Paul said. "When people came, I guess they thought they were going to see something pretty sensual and racy, but it was just a movie that showed a man and woman in bed together talking most of the movie, with very little nudity. Sometimes we'd pack them in and sometimes we wouldn't draw flies. That's just the way the theater business is."

When was business best during the Paul/Catherine Ritchey era?

"Probably the longest-running movie we showed was 'Butch Cassidy and the Sundance Kid,' " Paul said. "That movie was a sleeper and we were able to get that film for a bargain and had big crowds. I think that ran for 17 or 18 weeks. I remember one night in particular, the line stretched way down to the firehouse on the corner, and I had to go out and tell those people they might as well go home and come back another night because there was no way I was going to be able to fit them in."

For the Ritcheys, there were many humorous incidents, too, over the years. Like the night the projectionist came downstairs for a coffee break, wandered around and relaxed a bit, then returned upstairs to the projection booth to find that the takeup reel wasn't working and the film was spilling all over the floor and out the door.

"Then there was the night we had a bat loose and flying around inside the theater," Catherine Ritchey said with a laugh. "It was a small bat, of course, but flying around in front of the projector, it looked huge and it had people scared and screaming."

On another occasion, the film distributor made a mistake which caused Paul Ritchey some embarrassment.

"Movies back in those days were composed of five or six 18-minute reels that you put on in sequence," he said. "One night, I had a movie going for about an hour and had shown the first three segments, and I went to change the film on schedule. All of a sudden, instead of part four of whatever the movie was, there was part of a Charlie Chan movie up on the screen that had nothing to do with the movie. The distributor had given a reel from a different movie!"

Catherine Ritchey remembers the many kids at the matinees on Saturdays -- one kid in particular.

"One time I was tending the concession during one of the Lassie movies. The movie was just about over, and a little boy came into the lobby crying his eyes out," she said. "I asked what was the matter and he said, 'Lassie's dying!' I gave him a bag of candy and told him to go back in and that by the time he finished the candy, Lassie would be OK again."

Overall, Paul and Catherine Ritchey have nothing but good things to say about their years in the business. They admit, however, that it can be a hard way to make a living.

"It looks like an easy business, and when people are coming through the door and buying tickets, it IS an easy business," Paul said. "But when they aren't coming through the door, it gets pretty tough."

Catherine agreed.

"If you own a theater, there are going to be many nights when only five or six people come to see your movie," she said. "But you've got to show it anyway."

Ahhhhh, the Scotia Theater. Scotia Theatre. Scotia Art Theater. Scotia Cinema. By whatever name you want to call it, it's an important piece of Dear Old Scotia. Wouldn't you agree?

Suddenly I have this great urge for a bag of buttery, salty popcorn. I think I'll ask Mary Carol if she wants to go down to the theater tonight!

Scotia Cinema, from the east, on a bright morning in 2004. (Alan Hart photo.)

PART II

Barbers and Bakers

There are enduring memories, I am sure -- regarding barber shops and bakeries of Scotia -- for anyone who grew up in Scotia during the latter half of the 20th century.

Barber shops. Boy, do I remember how important it seemed -- in the days when I was a teen-aged boy -- to get a nice, clean haircut every couple of weeks. You always got it cut toward the end of the week, maybe Thursday afternoon, because on Friday you shined your black shoes like new, put on your best white dress shirt, got your best pair of pants cleaned (at home or at the dry cleaners) to look your absolute, sharpest best for the date you were going on or the dance you were attending in hopes of dancing with that special new someone.

And Scotia had plenty of barber shops and barbers from which a fellow could choose in the 1950s, 1960s and 1970s.

The same was true of bakeries.

M-m-m-m-m. Bakeries. When you were a kid at your mother's side, there was nothing quite like walking into a bakery knowing that your mom is going to walk out the door with a cake, pie or cupcakes. All those items looked so good behind all those windows, and when you walked into the store and smelled them, they looked even better, didn't they?

Just as with barber shops, Scotia had no shortage of fine bakeries in the mid-to-late 1900s. We didn't have to rely on the supermarkets or even the Freihofer's wagons (do I dare date myself here and mention the horse-drawn wagons? The last year for the horse carriages was 1957) for our fresh, delicious baked goods in Scotia.

Personally, with both barbers and bakers, I was always pretty fickle as a kid and teen as to my loyalty as a customer, and I have

19

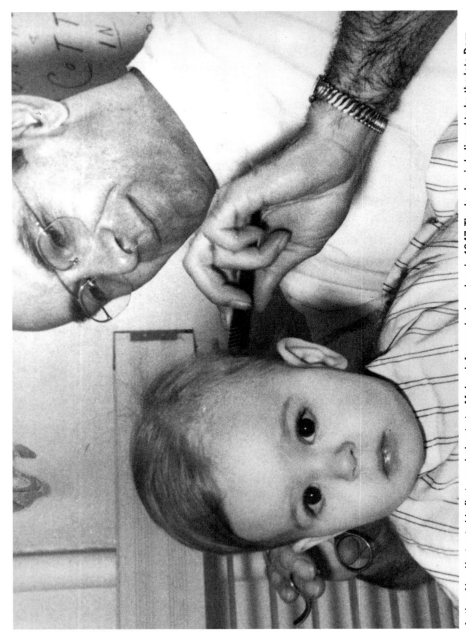

Author Alan Hart gets his first-ever haircut at a Mohawk Avenue barber shop in 1947. The barber is believed to be the late Dom Nicolella. (Larry Hart collection.)

continued that trend through adult life. What I mean is, when I need a haircut (mostly I get my neck shaved these days; there's little hair to bother with), I get it cut wherever I might happen to be at the time -- especially if I don't have to wait. Similarly, with bakeries I patronize a store whenever I need something and it has what I want or require, and I happen to be in that area.

Patience has never been my strong suit, as everyone who has ever known me more than casually will certainly attest. My friend Blase Iuliano, Saratoga High's longtime, legendary football coach, has a sign in his office which reads, "Lord, grant me patience ... and I want it right now!" I ought to have one of those signs around my neck.

First, when it comes to barbers, when I was a child and young teen growing up on Sanders Avenue, I usually got my haircuts at Gemmette's on Mohawk Avenue at the foot of Sacandaga Road. Why? Well, when I was a boy, that was where my mother took me most of the time, so I kind of got used to the barbers there as an older boy and a teen. There were three or four barbers working there in the 1950s and early 1960s, and my favorite was a friendly Italian fellow named Dom DaMassa. He lived on outer Sacandaga Road near my friend, Rose Gerardi, and he was a great talker. (Sadly, DaMassa, who later had a shop of his own next to what is now Ken Hughes' CPA business on Mohawk Avenue, passed away some years ago as a young man.)

But I didn't always go to Gemmette's. If there was a crowd in there, I walked further down the street to some other shop. Sometimes I went to Vern's, operated by Vern Foster. First he was in a shop down on the corner of Reynolds Street and Mohawk, then he moved way down to the Collins Park end of Mohawk. Boy, little did I know back then that the same man who occasionally cut my hair there during my crazy teen years would sometimes be trimming my thinning, graying strands -- at that same Mohawk Avenue shop -- now that I'm 57.

Bakeries? If you lived in Scotia in the years in which I describe, you know the joy I'm talking about when you walked

This photograph was taken in front of Daniel Henry "Grandpa" Slover's home at 212 Mohawk Avenue circa 1910. The former home is now the site of Style's Men's Hair Studio. Slover's children, from left, on the porch are Rosella, Elma, Cora, Caroline, Roy and Edith. (Larry Hart collection.)

into the old Hometown Bakery on Mohawk Avenue. The owner and baker, Arnold Wakker, was a master at his craft.

My mouth still waters at the mere thought of something which he baked that was called Rice Rolls. Remember? He also made Rice Bread, which obviously was another shape of the same thing, but those rolls were truly awesome. You could pick one up and enclose it in your palm like a baseball cut in half, but it had a kind of burnt, crusty layer on top that was the secret to it all. If you were lucky, you could get a bag of them while they were still warm and sneak one out of the bag on the way home and eat it plain. You didn't need butter on one of those rolls. They had enough taste of their own; you didn't need to amplify it.

Hometown Bakery was not the only Heaven-on-Earth in Scotia for people who loved baked goods. How about the Dutch Oven on the corner of Vley Road and Fifth Street? (It also was called Davidson's at one time.) If you want to talk about the best doughnut you ever ate in your life, if you are like me your mind will race back to a time when you were a younger person and you went to the Dutch Oven and bought a jelly doughnut with white frosting, or a cream-filled doughnut with chocolate topping, or a cinnamon twist.

Of course, in my boyhood days on Sanders Avenue I was spoiled with the stuff you could order right from the Freihofer man who stopped every day around 11 or 12 o'clock with the horse-drawn wagon (and then the small truck, after 1957.) I mean, as a kid you LIVED for those chocolate cup cakes with the white cream centers. Or the cylinder-shaped doughnuts with the coconut covering (they had a name, but I can't remember what they were called.) And let's not forget those delectable "Party Cupcakes" that were tiny, two-or three-bite cakes that were half frosting. If it was winter, they tasted even better because the frosting would be almost frozen. Yum! (To this day, I think the Thin Mint cookies the Girl Scouts sell taste best if you keep them in the freezer and eat them cold.)

Hey ... why am I sitting here writing? I'm going to go get a sweet snack. In the meantime, listen to what some other people have to say on the subject of barber shops and bakeries, OK? See you in a few.

* * *

Vern Foster

I had the distinct privilege of sitting in Vern's Barber Shop one late February afternoon in 2004, at the end of Foster's workday.

There Vern Foster and Paul Grippo, one of Foster's longtime customers and best friends, sat in chairs near the front window of the shop. They looked out on Mohawk Avenue and beheld many people going about their business -- some heading home from work during the rush hour, others perhaps on an errand of some sort.

Many of those persons Foster was watching have probably, at one time or another, had their hair cut by Foster, a fixture in the Village of Scotia. Foster, a native of the tiny community of Salem in Washington County, has been working at his trade in Scotia for 48 years.

"I can't imagine doing anything else than being a barber here in Scotia," said Foster, a very friendly man with a full head of white hair. (There's an old saying never to trust a bald barber because he has no respect for your hair. No problem here with Foster.)

"I went to the Royal Academy of Barbers in Schenectady above Rudnick's in 1952. When I was drafted in March of 1953 I went in the service, and when I got out I worked for Rocky's Barber Shop on upper Union Street in Schenectady. But then I took a job at George's Barber Shop down on the corner of Reynolds and Mohawk in 1955. I was there for two and a half years and then I bought this place in 1957 from Antoine Pintievalle, and I've been here ever since. I have absolutely no plans to retire, because this is what I like to do. Besides, my wife wouldn't have it any other way."

Foster was referring to Rosemary, his wife of 31 years.

According to Foster, in 1957 Scotia had seven barber shops and 17 barbers. Times have changed. Today, Scotia has two barber shops (not counting unisex establishments) and two barbers. Many barber shops simply went out of business during the 1970s because men tended to wear their hair longer and needed a haircut only a few times a year.

"What I did then was go into hair styling and hair replacement, and that kind of kept me going in the days when guys weren't getting the flat-top haircuts anymore," Foster said with a laugh. "I've cut a lot of people's hair here, but my favorite customers are the kids. I love doing little boys' haircuts. Sometimes their moms will come in and offer to stand there beside their boy in case he fusses, but I tell them there's no need. I have Smokey the Bear."

How's that?

Foster went to his counter and picked up a small figurine of the famous bruin firefighter to show Grippo and the interviewer.

"I let them hold Smokey the Bear while I tell them a story about Smokey, and before you know it the haircut is done," the grinning, bespectacled Foster said. "There are customers I have who are 35 or 40 years old who come in here and know about Smokey the Bear, because I've been using Smokey for 46 years now."

Grippo, who retired a few years ago after a long career with Schenectady County in highway maintenance, reminded Foster of the time that Foster -- who is something of a prankster -- played a joke on one of their mutual friends, Marty Campbell Sr.

Foster nodded and giggled when reminded of the prank.

"Marty came in one day in a hurry and said his wife wanted him to get a fresh haircut because they had an important PTA meeting that night," Foster said. "Well, I gave him a good haircut all right, but I left a square patch of full hair on the back of his head, and I didn't tell him. He came back the next day and he was pretty mad at me! We were always playing tricks on each other in those days."

One thing that is no joking matter with Foster is the sport of golf. He loves it. In fact, it is fair to say that, with Foster, golf is more of a passion than a sport. A license plate on the wall of his shop reads: WHOLEN-1.

Foster for the past 25 years has been a member of the Stadium Golf Club on Jackson Avenue in Schenectady. He plays there nearly every morning of the summer before coming to work.

"I tee off with Lou King, my main golfing buddy, every summer day right around 5:15 in the morning," Foster said. "Then I come in and get started here around 8 o'clock. Usually in the summer I take my last appointment at 2 o'clock, so I'm back out on the course at 4 o'clock -- if I want to."

Foster is a longtime supporter of Scotia's high school sports teams, particularly the boys' basketball team. (He is himself a former basketball/baseball standout at Salem.) He lends support to other school activities as well. If you want proof, check out his collection of Scotia high school yearbooks on display in his shop for customers to browse through while awaiting their turn in the chair. The collection runs consecutively from 1933 through to the present, but there also are other yearbooks from 1909, 1911 and 1913.

"I've always loved Scotia," Foster said. "When I was a high school junior in Salem, my mom moved here when she remarried. My stepfather worked for GE," Foster said. "Scotia just grew on me, and I jumped at the chance to work here when the chance came. Scotia is a beautiful place with its streets, the lake and the park. But it's not just the place that makes it beautiful; it's the people."

Grippo nodded his head in agreement.

"Especially on a summer day, you can always find something to do in Scotia," Grippo said. "You can go down to Collins Park at 8 in the morning and spend the whole day there."

And just a few steps away from the park, a fellow can get a

haircut there, too. Just don't drop in too long after 2 p.m., because the barber shop will be closed and there will be a sign on the door that says, "Gone Golfing."

* * *

Bakeries? Everybody who lived in Scotia during the 1950s and 1960s seems to remember the Hometown Bakery on Mohawk Avenue. The former bakery site is now an optical goods store.

"I sure DO remember Wakker's (bakery)," said Sharon (Hartley) Dunlap, now a Schenectadian who grew up on James Street in Scotia right behind the First Baptist Church. "Gwen Wakker (baker's daughter) was one of my best friends throughout my school years, and when I stayed over at her house, her father would always bring home jelly doughnuts for us."

Longtime village resident Tony Dorazio Sr. smiles at the mention of rice rolls and rice bread from Wakker's.

"Arnold used to make those delicious rice rolls for our Rotary meetings," Dorazio said. "When he moved away, he gave me some rice bread to keep, and I froze it. We've eaten most of it now, but I still have some stored away in the freezer."

Anyone who lived in Scotia during the 1950s and 1960s knew they had great baked goods available at Wakker's "Hometown Bakery" on Mohawk Avenue. The building now is the site of a store for optical needs and goods. (Larry Hart collection.)

Part III

Schools: Some are Gone, Some Remain

Ahhhhh. School days. Remember them? Everyone has sweet memories of days gone by when you had some of the best friends you would ever have in your life. And you spent maybe 12 hours a day, including classes in school, alongside them sometimes -- walking to and from school, playing sports, buying a fudgesicle or a soda at a store on the way home (even in the winter), hanging out, having fun.

Of course, there was the real WORK of school: the homework (yuck!), the exams and, even worse, the "unfair" pop quizzes that always caught you (me, at least) totally unprepared and brought your grades down. Most people, I guess, look back at this period of their lives and say, "Wow, that was a great time in my life. I LOVED it."

Well, I kind of vacillate on this issue, because while I liked elementary school (the last five years at Sacandaga School) and my two years of junior high very much, I didn't care very much at all for high school. Do you remember Paul Simon's hit song "Kodachrome" which begins "When I think back on all the crap I learned in high school, it's a wonder I can think at all?" As far as I'm concerned, Rhymin' Simon couldn't have stated it better. That's exactly how I feel about those years I spent in Scotia High-- for the most part, anyway. I hated my first two-plus years of high school. I absolutely loathed those freshman and sophomore years. Things did get better the last two years. (More on this later in the chapter.)

But let's start in the beginning (not MY beginning, Scotia's beginning) as it applies to education.

An important note here: For much of the factual matter which will appear in this chapter, I refer to papers from my late father

Larry Hart's personal files as Schenectady County historian. The reference paper was entitled "History Markers of Scotia Schools."

EARLY SCHOOLS

Scotia's first school of any sort was an old schoolhouse on Sacandaga Road. It was approximately 24-foot square and built in 1818 at a cost of $250. There was one teacher, and that person earned a salary that year of $210 for a nine-month school year. Eventually, that was ripped down and another schoolhouse -- this time made of brick -- was built on the same site in 1843 at a cost of $600. It was the only school in the village until 1870 when a new brick building was constructed on Mohawk Avenue adjacent to the First Baptist Church at a cost of $1,800. The school -- which would in time be called "Old"

The Mohawk Avenue School was a familiar sight in Scotia from its construction in 1870 until it was demolished in 1962. The school was converted into an ice cream plant in its later years and also sat abandoned before it was removed and made into a parking lot. (Larry Hart collection.)

Mohawk School -- later became the Colonial Ice Cream Plant. The building was torn down on April 5, 1962, and is now a parking lot and open space.

I do not remember the old Sacandaga Road schoolhouse, of course. It was long gone by the time I was born in November of 1946. But I do remember very well the Colonial ice cream building which had been "Old" Mohawk School. I used to walk past it going to and from Sunday services with my mom and dad and sister at the Baptist church. It struck me as a queer, abandoned old building that was pretty spooky-looking.

This photo (circa 1910) taken from the old water tower on Second Street shows a southeastern view of the Scotia landscape at the time, including old Placid Hall (foreground) of St. Joseph's Church. In the center is the old school which originally served as the village's high school when it was built in 1905 at a cost of $20,000. It was used as a junior high (seventh grade) building in its later years before it was razed in January of 1976. (Larry Hart collection.)

FIRST STREET JUNIOR HIGH SCHOOL
(Also Known in the late 1950s as "The Seventh-Grade Building")

This building, originally the high school, was built in 1905 at a cost of $20,000 to house grades 9 through 12.

The school year which I spent there, though, was September of 1958 to June of 1959. I certainly remember it, too.

Why? I guess for the simple reason that there obviously were more demands put on my time -- schoolwork-wise -- and suddenly there were less hours to spend as one pleased. The schoolwork, obviously, was much, much harder than what had been expected of us kids in elementary school. (Mathematics, never a subject for which I had any use even as a child, suddenly became my life-long nemesis and enemy in seventh grade. To this day, I struggle each month to figure out why the checkbook balance doesn't agree with what the bank says it should!)

Still, there were many great times and fond memories of that Seventh-Grade Building, though I only spent one year there. The "Teen Town" dances on Friday night were fun. I didn't do much dancing -- except for slow dances with "special" girls to tunes like Ricky Nelson's "Lonesome Town." Truthfully, I probably spent less time in the small gym and on the dance floor than I spent upstairs in the rec room buying cokes, playing ping-pong and hanging out with Russ Hawkins, Dan Friedlander, Bruce Holmwood and other guys.

I remember -- and I am sure everyone else who went there remembers -- the creaky floors, the cramped rooms, the noisy, hissing heaters. Sometimes if you were in a class on the first floor and the class on the second floor above you was dismissed before yours was, you'd swear the kids were going to fall right through the ceiling above you and crash down on your head. Remember the fire escape climbs? How about going down to the basement classrooms for music -- with Mr. Moser, and reading -- with Mr. Thorn?

There were those nice walks over to the Eighth-Grade

Building for gym class and special assemblies. Man, you looked forward to that, just to get outside and get away from the classrooms for an hour or so.

Whereas the Eighth-Grade Building (we'll get to it in a minute) survived the wrecking ball and is still a part of the community today (as the Schenectady Christian School), the Seventh-Grade Building was demolished during the winter of 1975-76. But it is not forgotten. I'm not the only person who remembers.

Witness:

Sharon (Hartley) Dunlap remembers going to seventh grade there in 1959-60.

"I loved that school ... the way the floors above you creaked -- the small rooms," Dunlap said. "It was fun when we walked to the big building -- the Eighth Grade Building -- for an assembly or something."

Clarence Langley, who taught seventh-grade science and mathematics for many years in that building during his long

The old First Street School meets the wrecking ball in January of 1976. (Photo by Woody Woodworth, Scotia-Glenville Journal.)

The freshman class of Scotia High (First Street School) is pictured on Oct. 6, 1916. Identifiable persons in the photograph are as follows: First row, from left: John Heckler, Earl Button, Neil Reynolds, Lawrence Dougall, Clifford Palmer, Arpad Vargas, Lewis Dunn. Second row, from left: Ivar Tans, Philip Dalton, Kenneth Brundige, William Gillespie, Albert Weir, Alexander Jacobson, Howard Compton, Grant Tymerson, Harold Heritage, Ernest Van Huysen, Milton Lansing, ?, Milton Nethaway. Third row, from left: Magdalene Stephens, Gertrude Lockrow, Helen Crippin, Nellie Bunnell, ?, Mildred Ryney, Florence Buhrmaster, Marion Putnam, Mary Tymerson, ? Fourth row, from left: Mary Matthews, ?, Gladys Toft, Anna Brown, ?, Lillian Lasher, Hazel Woodworth, Marion Patrick, ?, Carrie Fenton, Ebba Asp, Evengeline Baldwin, Winifred Levy, Cordelia Lewis. (Photo courtesy of Joan Szablewski.)

34

career, smiles widely when he recalls an incident involving what he thought was a fire drill. The incident illustrates the dry wit of Langley -- something he has retained from his teaching days.

"I had just started teaching there, and one autumn morning during one of my classes a strange bell started clanging," Langley said. "I stuck my head out in the hall and saw Mr. (Stephen) Baldwin -- the art teacher -- and asked what the bell meant. Turns out he was the wrong one to ask! He said, 'I believe it's the fire alarm!' So ... we both led our classrooms full of kids out onto First Street. After we were all standing out there for a few minutes we suddenly realized that the rest of the people in the school had stayed inside -- because it wasn't a fire drill at all, it was an air raid drill."

What happened next?

"Dr. Donald Friedrichs -- the principal -- came out to First Street where I was standing, and he was pretty mad. He got closer to me and yelled, 'What the sandhill are you and all these kids DOING out here?' " Langley said. Then Langley chuckled as he remembered his wise-guy reply of, "We're out here protecting all you cowards in there from the bombs!"

Bucky (Tony Jr.) Dorazio remembers that school because of a bombshell of another kind -- an attractive young teacher.

"That year for homeroom I had a teacher named Miss Spencer," Dorazio said. "She was fresh out of college, maybe 22 years old, and I thought she was stunningly beautiful. I couldn't wait to get to school every day!"

OLD HIGH SCHOOL ON SECOND STREET
(Also Known in the late 1950s as the Eighth-Grade Building)

This building, of course, located on Sacandaga Road and taking up the entire block across the street from St. Andrew's Episcopal Church, originally served as Scotia High School before the present Scotia-Glenville High School opened in 1958. The building now serves as Schenectady Christian School.

The Scotia High School class of 1949 makes its way up the stairway in the old gymnasium. Identifiable in the photograph (not in order) are: George Bull, Dick Carnwright, Bob Brown, Lois Dunn, Marilyn Hampel, Barrent Henry, Hedwig Dworakoolski, Nancy Finch, Bailey Markham, Warren Daniels, Barbara Cranston, Joyce Fallon, Clyde Colborn, Ronald Galster and instructor Len Proschel. The building in succeeding years became the Junior High (Eighth Grade) and has since become Schenectady Christian School. (Larry Hart collection.)

Construction of the building began in 1923. Architect of the building was J.M. Ryder, and it was finished -- and dedicated -- in 1925. Total cost? It was $340,000.

Like anyone else, I guess, when I started eighth grade at this school in September of 1959, I felt like a "big kid" again. You know how it is when you're going through elementary school and you FINALLY get to sixth grade, why, you're one of the big kids. Then you go to seventh grade and suddenly the tables are turned again: you're one of the younger kids, looking up to the eighth-graders -- many of whom had had a major growth spurt and seemed much older than a year older than yourself. But in eighth grade, ahhh ... you're a big kid again, if only for a year. (Because in ninth grade you're on the bottom of the student food chain again.)

Memories of eighth grade? I have a ton of them. Again, the work seemed very demanding, as one would expect. I remember most of all working my tail off -- during the spring months -- on a Social Studies project for a big, tall and friendly teacher named Mr. Schwarting -- on the state of Alabama. Each student had to pick a state other than New York State and do an extensive report on that state: its history, commerce, politics, tourism ... you name it. I remember working on that stupid thing during most of what would otherwise have been a nice Easter vacation week in April. (Note: I DID get a good grade on it, though, and to this day I can tell you about the Tennessee Valley Authority, then-Gov. John J. Sparkman and how he once ran for vice-president but lost, and all about a pretty flower called the azalea.)

My favorite memory of that building -- not of eighth grade but of that building -- has to be playing recreation basketball (for the Methodist church team and a high school rec team) in that gymnasium. The locker room was a floor above the gym, and then you went down the stairs to the floor. It was a noisy place to play, and it was great! At the north end, there were more stairs which led to a flat area where Mr. Dick Rollins -- our gym teacher -- always had ping-pong tables set up. (I remember competing in an open tournament there that spring. One of my good buddies, Jon Horstmann, knocked me out in the first round!)

A "scary" memory -- but also a good one -- was singing in a barber shop quartet (along with Dennis Madden, David Steel and Bob Glywa) during a special Thanksgiving assembly in that old auditorium there with the wooden seats with the curved backs. Mr. (later Dr.) Henry Sullivan, our music teacher and chorus director that year, approached us four boys about singing a special song. It was called "It's You" (from the musical "The Music Man"), and when Mr. Sullivan bounced the idea off of us that day, it seemed like a pretty good idea at the time. But that fateful morning we walked out on the stage around 11:30 a.m. to sing and all the other hundreds of kids in the audience were waiting and staring at us, I remember the lump in my throat, the shaking of my knees and the sudden still, small voice inside me screaming at me "Alan, what the hell are you DOING?! Why are we out here?! Are you crazy?!" But David blew the pitch pipe to get us on key, and then we started singing, and soon it was over. I managed, somehow, to hit that very high note -- which I had to hit as high tenor -- at the very end of the song. From that morning on, right to this day, I never again have been afraid to sing, speak or preach in front of an audience. I owe that to Dr. Sullivan, and also to Dennis, David and Bob.

Of her one year in this Eighth-Grade Building as a junior high student, Sharon (Hartley) Dunlap remembers most of all her history teacher.

"Early in the year, our teacher Mrs. (Bertha) Lee had to go on maternity leave," Dunlap recalled. "To take her place, we got a new, young teacher named Mr. (Larry) Rainey. We girls thought he was very handsome, and he was a very good teacher. Mr. Rainey eventually wound up in the high school in the years I was up there, too."

SCOTIA-GLENVILLE HIGH SCHOOL

The current high school on Sacandaga Road (Route 147) took awhile to move from the architect's drawing board to actual construction. The school, on a 27-acre site between Sacandaga Road and Sacandaga Elementary School, was first proposed in 1951. After a series of legal battles, construction on the new school eventually got underway in November of 1956. Students in grades 9 through 12 finally walked through the doors in September of 1958.

Tony Dorazio Sr. remembers how it came about that the school came to be built on land which used to belong to his family.

"My father (Alexander Dorazio) and John Henry Buhrmaster -- J.H., we called him -- were very good friends," Dorazio said. "Then Ken Buhrmaster, J.H.'s son, was president of the school board in the late 1950s. My father owned that land on which the high school and all the various athletic fields there rest now, and Dad had planned to develop that land with homes. But Ken approached Dad one day in a friendly, neighborly way. Ken told him he realized what plans he envisioned, but that the village kids needed a new school, and the school board believed Dad's land was the best place to put the school and would he consider making it a school instead. I don't know the full details of how the deal was made, but basically Dad said, 'The school is more important than homes. We'll go for it.' "

Do you remember me telling you how much I disliked most of high school? I wasn't kidding. I hated my freshman and sophomore years.

Part of the reason for this was because -- I know now in hindsight -- I was very immature and just didn't "get it," if you know what I mean. But in my own humble defense, I will say right here that everyone has certain ages in their lives where they start to question things and they say, "Why me?" That is to say, why am I not as attractive as other people, or not as athletic or as talented? For Alan Hart, age 14 and 15 were those years. That confused teen-ager who used to walk around in my body took a bit longer to "wise up," if you will, than most kids. That's why those first two years were rough ones. I made them rough with my own stupidity and stubborn nature.

I racked up the bad grades to prove that immaturity, stupidity and stubborn nature, too. Worse yet, I was getting "unsatisfactory reports" (remember those?) in between the bad quarterly report cards themselves, and they were even worse than the bad report cards because teachers (many of whom knew my mother, since she was a teacher at Sacandaga School) would make disparaging comments on them like "Alan isn't paying attention in school and is not applying himself. He doesn't seem to care." Know what? They were right! I hated school.

A famous college and pro basketball coach (I think it was P.J. Carlesimo) once had a talented player on his team who ought to

Ground for the new (and current) Scotia-Glenville High school on Sacandaga Road is finally broken on Nov. 26, 1956. High school principal Donald Letts, fourth from right, and school superintendent William Martin, second from right, were on hand for the ceremony. Work then soon began in earnest as construction got underway that winter. (Larry Hart collection.)

have been one of the best players in the nation but instead was a huge disappointment. The young man made no attempt to learn the defensive schemes or the set offensive plays this coach had implemented into the system. One day, the coach stopped his practice right in the middle of a drill and called the troublesome player over. He asked him, "Son, what the hell is your problem? Is it that you aren't quite intelligent enough to understand what I'm asking you to do out there, or is it your attitude that you just don't want to do what I tell you?" The kid looked him straight in the eye and answered, "Coach, I don't know and I don't care!"

Academically, I pretty much was just like that stubborn basketball player in ninth and 10th grade at Scotia High with teachers, tests, homework and classes. I didn't want teachers bothering me; I didn't want their help and I certainly didn't want their grief.

Let me give you an example, OK? This is one of my most vivid high school memories:

I was failing Elementary Algebra in ninth grade in early October of 1960. Already I was hopelessly behind the rest of my class with no light at the end of the tunnel. I knew it, and so did my "battleaxe" of a teacher -- Miss Dickson. (The late Miss Margaret Dickson, of course, was no battleaxe, but I couldn't stand her and I don't think she was wild about me, either.) Anyway, one particular October morning she began class by passing out the most recent weekly test she had given a day or two earlier. My test, of course, had another failing grade at the top in red pen. When she placed mine on my desk, she said to me in a stern voice, "Young man, I want to see you here after school today to begin taking some review classes. You're not picking up the material; you're not keeping up with the rest of the class."

That, believe it or not, was a masterpiece of understatement. I didn't have a clue what she was talking about in class, nor did I care.

I didn't say anything then, but when the period was over I boldly walked right up to her and said, "Miss Dickson -- sorry, but there's no way I'm staying after school today with you for extra instruction. No way."

Startled and clearly annoyed, she asked me why. I said, "Because today is Game Seven of the World Series. I have to go home and see the end of the game. I can't miss it!" (To you young readers, the World Series was played exclusively in the afternoon in those "olden days.")

This made perfect sense to me. Stay for extra math work? Why, I was a rabid baseball fan, for Heaven's sake. (Still am!) The New York Yankees and Pittsburgh Pirates were dead even at three wins apiece, and this game would decide the championship! (I was a Yankee fan then until the expansion New York Mets came along in 1962.)

Flabbergasted at how my priorities were -- to her way of thinking -- way out of line, Miss Dickson's face flushed bright red, and she snapped back at me with, "What's more important, young man: algebra or the World Series?"

Equally flabbergasted at Miss Dickson's reaction, my jaw fell and I said, "Well, that's a dumb question. The World Series, of course!"

I meant it, too.

I didn't go to her review class that day. Nope. Instead, I saw Bill Mazeroski hit the walk-off home run to give the Pirates the championship.

I got a "D" that quarter in Algebra. In fact, I got a "D" all four quarters. Believe it or not, that was pretty good compared with how I did in Geometry the following year. (After failing that class as a sophomore, I had to repeat Geometry in my junior year. By then I was a more attentive, mature and responsible student ... finally. Still, I only got a 71 on the Regents the second time!)

Ahhh, high school. Many people say it was the best time of their life. Not me. But, at least I got through it.

As I said before, I loved the sports teams I played on (more on that in ensuing chapters.) Also, I enjoyed most -- but not all -- of my experience of being a four-year member of the Choralaires --

the select chorus founded and still directed at that time by the late Mr. Carl Steubing.

There were other high school teachers, too, who made a tremendous impact on my life. At the top of the list is Karl-Heinz Gerstenberger, who was my soccer coach and German teacher in my senior year. Not once but twice Karl wrote a letter of recommendation for me to help get me into the University at Albany -- as an undergrad transferring from Hudson Valley Community College in 1966 and as a middle-aged man seeking to get a Master's degree in 1991. Both times, Karl came to the rescue. To this day, he is a treasured friend.

Then there was Dr. Sullivan -- the man who almost literally pushed that quartet I was a part of in junior high out on the stage -- who was such an inspiration in music. There were great (I thought) English teachers such as Mr. Robert Atwood and Mr. Thomas Gilmartin, who both inspired me to cultivate my writing skills.

I don't want to forget Mr. Fred Paul, either. He was a mathematics teacher who patiently guided me through a black forest otherwise known to other students as Intermediate Algebra and Trigonometry. Darn nice man, too.

And there were the baseball coaches, too -- JV coach Mr. Philip Bremser and varsity coach Mr. Cecil "Pete" Ellithorpe. They were good men to play for, and they knew their stuff.

High school. No, it wasn't the high point of my life. But there were good times -- especially in the last two years. If I had those first two years as a freshman and sophomore to do over again, I know I would do things differently this time. At the same time, I think I learned a lot from my mistakes of those years, so ... isn't that the same thing?

Other people, of course, loved every minute of high school in Scotia. Sharon (Hartley) Dunlap is a prime example.

"Really, the only sad year I had was my senior year, and that's because most of my friends were a year older than me and had already graduated. It was kind of a lonely last year there."

Dunlap recalls many, many happy days there, however.

"My boyfriend one year was Dennis Wagner, and he played in the band. I used to sit next to him at the football games out in the bleachers, and he used to let me wear that big, fuzzy hat the kids in the band used to wear. I loved going to the football games -- and the basketball games. Another year, my boyfriend was John Engel. He was a very talented artist. John is the one who made that mosaic display near the entrance. It's still there, today, so you can still see it."

"OLD" LINCOLN SCHOOL

This venerable, old building -- which was located on the north end of Fourth and Fifth Streets and Huston Street, was originally a four-room structure built in 1910 at a cost of $10,000. In 1912, four rooms were added at a cost of $12,000. It was razed on June 15, 1979, to make room for Holyrood House -- a six-story senior citizen housing facility.

I have little or nothing to add concerning this school from a personal standpoint. I never attended the school. I don't think I was ever inside the place.

"NEW" MOHAWK SCHOOL

OK, here's a school I can tell you things about. I lived right across the street from the side entrance to the school. (The main entrance was on South Ten Broeck Street.) I attended Kindergarten and first grade there before transferring to Sacandaga School for the rest of my grade school years (because my mother began teaching there in 1953, and naturally she wanted my sister Bonnie and me to be in the same school with her.)

Mohawk School was built in 1917 at a cost of $60,000.

Mohawk School's playground, as I mentioned in the preface, was a happy place teeming with active young people of all ages. It wasn't that large a playground, in retrospect, I guess. But it

The "Old" Lincoln School, at Huston Street and Fourth and Fifth Streets, was a popular place of learning in the village and served in a number of capacities from 1912 until 1979 when it was demolished to make room for Holyrood House -- a housing complex for senior citizens. The school served as an elementary school when this 1938 classroom photo was taken on school grounds. Identifiable students include: Front row, from left: Richard Heineman, Thomas Sweeney, Charles Pastore, ?, Donald Pickney. Second row, from left: Raymond Bowman, ?, Kenneth Sebis, Robert Metzger, Louis Isabella. Third row, from left: Carolyn Wheeler, ?, Marion Johnson, Mary Lou Talbot, Joan Spencer, Linnea Mellen, Julia Terry, ? Fourth row, from left: (Teacher), Marilyn Jesmain, Jane Abercrombie, ?, ?, Carol Whitmyer, ?. (Building photos from Larry Hart collection; class photo courtesy of Joan Szablewski.)

seemed like a prairie to a young kid -- which I was when I lived across the street. There was a ballfield on the south side of the playground along Riverside Avenue. If I had to guess now, I'd venture to say that I probably played 1,000 to 2,000 pickup games there with kids of all ages from the time I was old enough to swing a bat until I was 16 or so. More important, my fondest memory of my father is walking over to that field with him as a nine or 10-year-old so he could hit fly balls and grounders to me. (Our yard was too small for that.) That may not seem like that big a deal to you, but it is when you realize that not every dad in the world takes the time to do that with his son or daughter. Mine did.

We kids used to sneak in the school at night, too. It was easy. You'd take a stick or small tree branch and put it in the corner of one of the big, heavy doors at the Ten Broeck Street entrance so that the door wouldn't close all the way and lock. (Teachers and administrators walking out wouldn't even notice.) Then we'd sneak in at say, 8 or 9 o'clock when it was dark and spooky and walk and run around in the first-floor halls, maybe go in a classroom or two and toss a few blackboard erasers around ... nothing bad. We never did anything destructive. It was just harmless fun.

The Mohawk School building is still standing, but it is now a place where people make their homes in apartments and condominiums. The old playground is no more. The site is now taken up with more houses and apartments. The old, small cement basketball court -- where I used to watch older kids like Larry Matura, Bruce Oudt, Ken Hughes and Ted Van Allen play serious pickup games well past sunset until you couldn't see anymore -- is gone. The short right-field fence where I hit my first out-of-the-park homer anywhere (as a 10-year-old off of Russ Hawkins' older brother, Kenny) is gone.

Alas, old playground, goodbye.

SACANDAGA SCHOOL

Sacandaga, for which I can vouch was a great place to have been a kid trying to learn the Three R's (reading, writing and 'rithmetic) during the 1950s, was built on Schermerhorn Road and dedicated in 1931. Built at a cost of $232,000, Sacandaga had 18 classrooms, and an auditorium/gym which was the largest venue for a concert or sports event in Scotia. (The school system had acquired the area called Kinum Plot in 1928 for not only the school but also a playground and athletic field.)

"Sac" was -- and still is -- a wonderful place. The playground had not one but TWO ballfields, plus a brick building used by the high school athletic teams for locker and shower facilities (still in use today.) The north side of that little building was what we used for a game called "Two-court" in which you chose up sides and threw large rubber playballs at each other. If you were hit by one of the balls by an opposing team member, you were "out" and had to leave the game. If you caught the ball, he or she was out instead. Most of the time, you just tried to stay away from getting hit by a ball and you concentrated on picking up loose balls or catching balls that caromed off that brick wall so you could throw it at another opposing team member.

Great game, but in hindsight it strikes me that it was probably a pretty rough game for the girls to have to play. I think we boys tended to like it a lot more than the girls. No small wonder.

I remember so well getting to school early, because my mother had to be there long before the bus kids showed up. I remember staying well after school classes ended, too. This is when I got to be such good friends with Russ Hawkins because his father, Ken Hawkins Sr., was a sixth-grade teacher across the hall from Mom's room. In those years (1953 or so right up until we both graduated from high school in 1964), except for the summer months when the Hawkins family vacationed in Holderness, New Hampshire, when you saw either Russ or myself, you saw

No, Mrs. Quinlan's first-grade class at Mohawk School didn't always dress in funny outfits like this. It's just that on this occasion, it was time for the annual Halloween party on Oct. 31, 1951. Identifiable students in the photograph are as follows: First row, from left: ?, Raymond Boss, Floyd Barwig, ?, Alan Hart, Billy Vazal, ?, Joe Homer, Mike Brandow. Second row: only identifiable person is Gwen Wakker (fourth from right.) Third row: only identifiable students are Arthur Coolidge (extreme left) and Jackie Walsh (fifth from right with flowers in her hair.) Identifiable in top row are Kelly Chlopecki (third from left) and Tom Beebe (fourth from left.) (Larry Hart collection.)

the other most of the time. We were very close friends. Russ moved out of the area right after high school. We only keep in touch by mail nowadays.

GLEN-WORDEN, GLENDAAL AND "NEW" LINCOLN

These three "new" elementary schools were part of a $2,455,000 bond authorization that was passed (by a 77.4 percent vote) on April 3, 1951 to not only construct these three new schools in the now-centralized district called Scotia-Glenville Central Schools but also to make upgrades on Sacandaga, Mohawk, the bus parking garage and to build the new high school.

It took awhile before ground was broken on any of these projects, but ... all three schools -- and the new high school -- finally became a reality. All three "new" elementary schools are still in use, as is Sacandaga.

* * *

Albert Moser Sr. is a master musician and dedicated educator who taught in nearly all of the above-mentioned schools in Scotia. Yet, if it hadn't been for a chance meeting in Hershey, Pa., early in 1953 with a symphony band director from old Mont Pleasant High School in Schenectady named Willard Musser, Moser might never have found his way to Scotia.

"It was my senior year at Lebanon Valley College in Pennsylvania, and I went to a concert that night to hear bands from different parts of the northeast," Moser said one sunny May 2004 morning at the breakfast table of his Marion Boulevard home. "I heard

Albert Moser

Sacandaga School was built in 1931 to serve the community as an elementary school, and it still is in use in that capacity. Behind the school to the west and north was Kinum's Woods, shown in this photo from March of 1937. (Larry Hart collection.)

this band from this school called Mont Pleasant, and I went backstage after the concert to congratulate Mr. Musser on the great sound his band was producing and how much I enjoyed it. We talked a little bit, and I told him I was a senior and a music major and asked him if there were any jobs available at his school. It turned out there were none at Mont Pleasant, but he knew of two in his area -- one in Altamont and one in a place called Scotia."

Another note of interest was that Musser knew Moser's father, Paul Moser, because they had played in a band together in Mt. Penn., Pa. -- a suburb of Moser's hometown of Reading. Albert Moser, who had married former hometown friend Peg Wentzel during his freshman year of college and was the father of six-month-old Albert Jr., was eager to find a teaching job that fall. He wrote letters and sent resumes to the superintendents of both the Altamont and Scotia schools that May.

Al and Peg Moser didn't hear anything for awhile, and they were starting to become discouraged. Then, one mid-August afternoon, they suddenly were on their way to Scotia.

"I was working in my in-laws' store and playing in some bands trying to make some money," Moser said. "Then one day I got a telegram from William Martin, Scotia's superintendent at the time. He said they had already filled the job in the high school that I had applied for, but would I be interested in working with elementary school-aged kids, teaching them music? I called him and told him I certainly would be interested. I drove to Scotia for an interview and I got the job, and I started that fall of 1953 teaching grade-school kids -- kindergarten through six grade -- at Mohawk and Sacandaga Schools."

Peg Moser smiles widely at the memory of the weekend they moved to the village -- the place which would become their home for at least the next half-century.

"We had an apartment in town and there were no screens on the windows, no fans and no air conditioning when we moved in. Those three days when we were moving and settling in, it was over 100 degrees each day. I'm not kidding ... when you see the weather reports every year in late August, they will always say that the record high for those dates was in 1953. Believe it!"

Albert and Peg Moser both are natives of Reading and attended the same church -- St. John's Reformed and Evangelical Church -- although they were just friends, not sweethearts, until they both were out of high school.

They began dating just before Albert's freshman year at Lebanon Valley College. Peg nodded and smiled again as Albert explained how he proposed marriage to her one day.

"I had an apartment that freshman year, and I shared it with another student named Theophilus Fish," Moser said. "We didn't exactly hit it off. He was always finding fault with me and we didn't like each other very much. Finally, one day I said to Peg, 'I can't stand my roommate. Let's get married.' "

Peg, giggling aloud at mention of this "romantic" proposal, said "Yes ... that's what he said. That's how he proposed to me. Can you imagine?"

The Moser marriage bond, however, has been a good and lasting one. So also was the Reading couple's decision to relocate in Scotia. After an enjoyable three-year tenure of teaching young children music and directing youth choirs, Moser was re-assigned to the junior high, where he taught more advanced music classes -- appreciation of classical, folk and modern music -- from 1956 through 1960.

Moser taught many young teens of Scotia the wonder of the sounds created by composers such as Gershwin, Stravinsky and Copeland. He taught them to recognize and enjoy the various sounds that band and orchestral instruments make.

"Teaching in the Seventh-Grade Building was an enjoyable time in my life," Moser said, smiling as he looked out a window into his backyard -- perhaps gazing not at the yard but at a fond memory of years past. "My classes were down on the basement floor, and it was kind of tough to teach there, to say the least. The shop class was next door, and that was loud sometimes with the various machines going. And the home economics class was right overhead on the first floor, and they had a washing machine up there that would sometimes overflow. The water would actually drip down through the floor and we'd have to move around to dodge the drips and puddles! Then there was a ladder going up to a window that we were supposed to be able to use to escape in case of a fire. And there were big pipes all over the ceiling. I used to worry that -- if there really were a fire -- if anybody could get out that way!"

As it turned out, the worry was short-lived. The school would soon be history, and not only those students of 1956-1960 but Moser himself would soon be moving up to the brand-new high school building and campus on Sacandaga Road.

"I left the music department in 1960 and started in the guidance department that September of 1960. I enjoyed teaching music, of course, but in order to be tenured as a teacher I had to get my Master's degree within five years, and if I wanted to get a Master's in music I had to travel to Potsdam to study whereas if I wanted to get the Master's in guidance and counseling, I only had to go to Albany State (now University at Albany), which of course was much closer and more convenient for me. I went summers, evenings, weekends ... and I got my Master's."

Moser eventually became chairman of the Guidance Department for a three-year stint. He retired in 1984 after 31 years as a teacher and administrator in the Scotia school system. He says they were wonderful years.

"Teaching music to those kids, as I look back on those years, was one of the most satisfying experiences I've had in music. Toward the end, though, around 1960 I knew I was making the right choice to go into guidance, because it seemed to me that the kids weren't as interested in music appreciation as kids of earlier years had been. It was like pulling teeth asking them to listen to classical and folk music. They wanted to hear Elvis Presley."

Moser soon felt at home with his new role in guidance.

"I was ready for something new, and I'm glad I went into

guidance. I thought, originally, I could do some music, too, but they wanted me to completely divorce myself from the music department, so that's the way that went. I enjoyed the counseling a lot more. Even though I also enjoyed teaching music, one day I realized, 'Hey, THIS is what I'm supposed to do.' I was there to see the whole transformation over from the old McBee Keypunch System of cards and files over to the computerized system. It was a very big improvement, and a much-needed one. It always used to be in the 'old days' before computers that there would be about 200 conflicts with classes for the kids. Even with all the advance preparation and scheduling we did during the summer, in September we'd have to call each student in one at a time and try to get their many conflicts resolved."

Still, it was music -- not guidance counseling -- which had a profound effect on reshaping another vital area of the lives of both Albert and Peg Moser. That area is religion. Moser is a perpetual deacon serving the Albany Episcopal Diocese. After being stationed at St. Andrew's Church in Scotia for over 30 years, Moser more recently has served at Christ Church in Ballston Spa. Peg, his staunch supporter in his many life ventures throughout their marriage, has been at his side for each move.

It all began in 1953, soon after that record-setting hot spell of August.

"We had both been raised in the Reformed church," Al Moser said. "When we first got here, Horace Peeling -- a teacher we both came to know right away -- invited us to the Reformed church in Scotia. But it wasn't quite what we were looking for. One day, though, there was a knock on our front door and it was Ruth and Horace Kelly, who introduced themselves as members of St. Andrew's. They said, 'We understand you're a new music teacher in the school system. We're looking for a person to be our organ player and choir director at $25 a month. Would you be interested?' "

The Mosers, who were looking not only for a church to attend regularly but also for a little extra money, were indeed interested. About 10 years later, Rev. William Gray -- priest at St. Andrew's from 1962 until 1987 -- asked Moser to consider aspiring to the diaconate as an ordained deacon. Moser, startled at first by the suggestion, agreed to begin studying the ministry. Moser had served as assistant chaplain in the Air Force at Hanada Base outside Tokyo, Japan from 1946 through 1949. It was at that base where he learned to play the organ.

"I was the troop's education and information officer there. The chaplain there asked me to assist him and play the organ and direct the choir. Well, I didn't really know how to play the organ, but I told him I could play piano, and he told me to do the best I could. I just started practicing -- playing the keys and pumping the pedals."

Moser, who has never had a lesson on playing organ, nonetheless is now recognized as one of the country's most accomplished pianists and organists. He gives an annual spring concert playing "Goldie" at Proctor's Theater in Schenectady and frequently plays for audiences there prior to screenings of motion pictures.

Moser is at home behind the keyboard of any organ or piano, and he is at home behind the altar and pulpit of an Episcopal church. But most of all, Albert -- and Peg -- Moser both feel at home in the village of Scotia.

It's the people who have made Scotia "home" to them.

"I have people come up to me -- at formal get-togethers or just at the gas station or store or something -- and they say, 'Aren't you Mr. Moser?' When I tell them yes, they will say, 'I had you for a teacher at Sacandaga School a long time ago,' or something like that. And it's always a gray-haired person with a grandchild. It makes me realize, then, how long ago that was and it makes me feel rather old. But I also appreciate that they remembered me after all those years, and that they'd take the time to walk up and say 'Hello.' "

* * * * * * *

SCHOOL SUPERINTENDENTS IN SCOTIA'S HISTORY
(Note: They were called "Supervising Principals" until 1918)

1905-14	E.A. Van Slyck
1914-17	J.B. Welles
1917-18	R. Weidler
1918-27	A.W. Miller
1927-49	B.W. Conrad
1949-69	W.H. Martin
1969-83	C.O. Eidens
1983-96	Patrick DiCaprio
1996-present	Michael Marcelle

Part IV
Good Things in Store(s)

If you lived in the village of Scotia in the latter half of the 20th century, you saw this community react to a cultural change that was occurring all over the nation -- the emergence of the large chain store and the mall.

The mall, with its obvious appeal of greater convenience (ample parking, everything you need in one centralized area), was usually anchored by one or two major stores and surrounded by many smaller ones.

Such shopping possibilities signalled the end of an era for many "Mom and Pop" stores all over the United States, and Scotia was not immune to this seismic metamorphosis in our culture. Many stores that had been in existence in the 1940s, 1950s and 1960s couldn't make a go of it once the malls started to spring up in Colonie, Rotterdam, Niskayuna and Clifton Park.

Since that time, it may have become still more difficult for private, independent stores to be successful going up against the large-chain K-Marts, Wal-Marts and Sears stores of the world.

Two glaring exceptions to this general dropoff in family-owned stores are to be found in Scotia -- Roy Matthews TV & Appliance Center on Mohawk Avenue and the Dorazio family's Wayside Hardware and Garden Center on Sacandaga Road. Both stores have survived the challenge of the big chain store in great style. These two stores have endured, and they both are true landmarks of the village.

Matthews' store, of course, used to be Swire's -- a department store in which one could purchase almost anything from appliances to clothes to toys to paint or hardware. Matthews himself was the personal bridge to the transition in name to a total appliance and media goods establishment in 1980, because he had been working at Swire's since he was a young teen in 1960.

Roy Matthews' TV and Appliance Center, shown in this photo from March of 1987, is a familiar part of Scotia's landscape. Its proprietor, Roy Matthews, worked at the building as a young teen-ager when it was Swire's Department Store. (Larry Hart collection.)

My own memories of Swire's are plentiful. How well I remember going in there with my mother and sister when I was a child, because while Mom would be shopping for clothing items in the spacious front room, my sister and I would be down in that toy section in the back where you walked down a ramp to find a wide selection of toys -- both pricey and inexpensive. There were small toys, big toys, books, marbles, toy western six-guns with "caps" ... you name it.

The most vivid memory I have of this store concerns the first nightmare or bad dream I believe I ever had. I don't know how old I was -- possibly four or five -- but I recall just such a visit to Swire's one afternoon with my mother and sister. Mom, who was in something of a hurry, said she would buy me one small item. I remember looking for the longest time at a toy snake, maybe six or eight inches long, that was in segments made out of something like cement or plaster and then painted green and other colors. Its mouth was open and painted red, and it had yellow and black eyes.

That toy snake was originally what I decided to get that day, but on the way to the counter (in the middle, next to the ramp) I spotted a bottle of soap with which you could blow soap bubbles. I suddenly changed my mind, and I put the snake back where I had found it. Well, that very night I woke up in the middle of the night dreaming that the snake I had chosen not to have my mother buy me was crying. I thought the snake, all alone in that dark store, was feeling bad because I hadn't bought him. So, I began to cry my eyes out because I felt bad for the snake. I remember Dad coming in to my room to find out what his son was blubbering about, and I doubt he understood what I was saying to him between sobs concerning "the poor, little snake." The story had a happy ending, though, because the very next time I was in that store, Mom bought me that toy snake.

Years later when I was a teen-ager, I remember seeing schoolmate Roy Matthews -- who is just about the same age as I am -- working at Swire's and thinking, "Man, he's got a job and he's

An elementary school class from Sacandaga School tours the old greenhouse at Wayside Hardware and Garden Center on a field trip in the 1960s. (Photo courtesy of Bucky Dorazio.)

making regular money. He's pretty ambitious. Good for him!" (Note: I didn't start working anywhere until I was 15 and worked in the summer picking green and yellow beans and pulling weeds at Ulrich's Farm down by the Mohawk River.)

That store, with its wooden floors, had a certain indescribable smell to it. It was not an unpleasant smell; it was more of a scent -- as in the way fresh lumber has an aroma in a lumberyard.

Dorazio's store? Gosh, how I remember going there for many years with my mother and father when they picked out plants and seeds for our small vegetable garden and for flowers for the backyard at 208 Sanders. Throughout my adult life, too, I have

Tony Dorazio handles plants in the greenhouse while his wife and co-owner, Charlotte, wraps a plant for a customer in these photos from July 1958. (Photos courtesy of Tony Dorazio.)

returned so many times to that store for hardware or yard items anytime a plumbing or outdoor chore requires a new tool or other product. (I used to buy my onion sets there every year, unfailingly, but the store no longer carries them.)

For so many years it was owned and operated by Tony Dorazio Sr. and his wife, the former Charlotte Buono. The establishment is now operated chiefly by their son, Tony Jr., who is better known as "Bucky."

The Matthews and Dorazio stores have not only endured but become landmarks of Scotia -- two places which come quickly to mind when one talks about the village and life in this community.

* * *

Roy Matthews

Roy Matthews at one time, in his younger days when he had wavy, black hair in a duck-tailed haircut, was a dead ringer for Elvis Presley. Indeed, when "The King" died in 1978, the insensitive joke around town was that Elvis hadn't died -- he had moved to Scotia and was living under an assumed name.

On a chillier-than-normal early April morning, however, Matthews (who now sports some telltale gray hair in that still-long mane of his) graciously took a few minutes -- between waiting on customers at the busy appliance store that has been his home away from home for 44 years -- to share some of his thoughts about his hometown.

"I think there's something special about Scotia ... I really mean that," Matthews said as he leaned over the counter of his store ... in an area right about where ladies' hosiery once was displayed for sale in the front half of old Swire's.

"My uncle, Harold Coons, always told me when I was getting started in this business, 'Stay home here where your roots are if you're going to own a store. Stay where people know you and support you.' Well, I did expand to have branch stores in South Glens and Colonie for awhile, but I eventually shut them down and just stayed here in Scotia. This is home, and I've been here for 25 years now."

Actually, Matthews has been at the Mohawk Avenue establishment in some capacity for 44 years. He was at the tender age of 13 when he got his working papers and got a job at Swire's.

"My mother, Leona Matthews, and my aunt, Eilleen Coons, both worked here in the early 1950s, and my grandfather (Roy Matthews) owned an insurance and real estate business here in town -- first across the street and then on Ballston Avenue," Matthews said. "My grandfather knew the owner here very well, and of course with Mom and Aunt Eilleen working here, they all kind of helped me get a job here. First they had me sweeping the floors and taking out the garbage, stocking shelves ... things like that. After awhile, I got to work at the counter."

In 1980 at age 33, Matthews -- who had remained a faithful and diligent worker at Swire's (for Bob Swire and his nephew, Tom Swire) for 20 years -- got the opportunity to work for himself instead of someone else.

"The store went out of business in 1979, and I had the chance to rent it . I wasn't sure I wanted to do that, because this was the heyday of the Big N, J.M. Fields and all those big stores. They were all thriving," Matthews said. "But I decided to take a shot at it, with the idea that I would feature only TVs, appliances and furniture. So ... I did it!"

Matthews admits it sometimes has been difficult to stay in business -- let alone be successful -- with the arrival of the big chain stores with which he has had to compete for the consumer dollar. Matthews, though, has survived because he has proven to be a shrewd businessman and a man who appreciates his customers.

"I don't have a secret. I just try to be honest with people. I think if I have a particular talent as a store-owner, it's that customers know most of all that if they have a problem with something I sell them, they know they can come back to me with the problem because I stand behind everything I sell. I'm not going to sell it to them and then forget about them. That keeps people coming back to you, so I guess if there IS a secret, that's it."

Matthews has another specific interest in his life: making sure that Vietnam veterans from his hometown are remembered. Matthews was instrumental, along with longtime friend Al Vrooman, in getting a memorial plaque placed in the lobby of Scotia-Glenville High School. On it are inscribed the names of six Scotia alumni who died in Vietnam. Two (Kenneth Fetter and David Vollmer) of the six who died were members of Matthews' graduating Class of 1966. The other four who died were Robert Jamro, Ronald Fero, Edward Malewicz and James McNeilly.

"I never served in the armed forces," he said. "But my dad served in World War II and my manager, Richard Parks, served in Vietnam. I just thought the kids who died for us in Vietnam never got the recognition they deserved, and I thought it would be a good idea to put the plaque in the high school so they would always be remembered."

It's a long way from Graceland, and Roy Matthews never has ventured far from his own hometown of Scotia -- in body or in spirit. The ongoing success of his store has rewarded his loyalty.

* * *

Bucky Dorazio

Bucky Dorazio smiled widely when asked about his family store's longevity. He was not around when it all began, but he speaks proudly of Wayside Hardware and Garden Center and obviously is pleased to be carrying on the work which his mother and father began.

"Originally, this was the family farm, started by my grandfather. In 1940, Dad started a fruit stand here out by the (Sacandaga) Road, and the farm was about 10 acres," Dorazio said inside his store one cold April afternoon.

Standing behind the counter, Dorazio pointed to his right.

"See that? That's the old part of the store -- the part with the sloped roof. That was the old part of the store when it first opened in 1945. Dad moved the fruit stand back off the road to where it stands now. Then he added on the rest of it later. He kind of blended it all together to make it look more modern."

Originally, the elder Dorazios -- Tony Sr. and Charlotte -- operated the fruit stand during the summer months, and Tony Sr. also worked for the Department of Public Works in the fall and winter months. Eventually, though, the Dorazio family decided to make the store a full-time venture.

"Dad had a lot of skill with plumbing and was handy with tools as a fix-it man," Bucky Dorazio said, his face beaming with pride. "He thought that if he could expand the business to include selling garden supplies and hardware, that he and Mom could make a go of it. Eventually, it evolved into what it is today -- a store with a wide variety of things that people want and need. Now, however, the store is about 85 percent hardware and 15 percent garden supplies. It used to be more even."

Bucky and his older sister (now Sandra Lannon) grew up watching the family business grow from its humble beginnings to the point where it became -- and has remained -- one of the most recognizable and familiar establishments in the village.

Funny, though: Bucky wasn't at all sure he wanted any part of the business ... at first.

"I always had it in my mind that I wanted to be a teacher," Dorazio said. "When I graduated from high school in 1972, I went off to Oswego State for four years and then I was a teacher for five years. I enjoyed it, but I also missed Scotia and the family. I just thought, too, that the business was too big for Dad alone, and I thought I could help."

The store, and the entire family, suffered a serious blow in 1990 when a fire destroyed the greenhouse -- one of the main attractions and money-makers of the business.

"That greenhouse used to be right in back here," Dorazio said, pointing behind the counter to a small room behind him. "The greenhouse was 60 feet long. But the fire took that right out. We built a separate greenhouse now that's much smaller -- about 40 feet long. Mom worked in that old greenhouse right up until the fire in 1990. Dad? He's still over here quite a bit, helping me with everything. This store is a big part of his life."

Bucky Dorazio said, truthfully, he never really wanted to leave Scotia in the first place because he thinks there's something special about the village.

"I know kids, when I was in high school, who hated Scotia. They couldn't wait to graduate and they couldn't get out of town quick enough," he said. "But you know what? I'm finding that those same people -- when they turned around 35 years old -- realized how nice life is here and they said, 'Why did I ever leave?' "

Like Roy Matthews, Bucky Dorazio credits sincerity and courtesy in dealing with customers as going a long way in his family's business.

"One of the things Dad -- and Mom -- taught me about this business is that it all boils down to personalized service and caring about people," he said. "Anyone who comes in here can get these items in other stores, but here you also get a lesson on how to do the job. You know that somebody is going to assist you and guide you if you have a question on a do-it-yourself job. I admit, it is difficult to compete with the big-box stores. There's no denying that it's more convenient for a customer to go to a big store where you can shop for everything you need under one roof and then pay for it all with a credit card. But you aren't going to get our kind of attention at a store like that. Service is what they want, and my family has always believed that people are entitled to that service."

Sometimes there are customers who push that Dorazio family courtesy to its limit. He smiled before relating just such an incident involving a dissatisfied customer.

"One time an older man came in here with a garden rake he had bought here three years earlier. He had used it to rake up leaves and sticks on his driveway and sidewalk, and all the teeth had been worn down right to the point where the bent parts of the teeth were completely gone," he said. "The man told me the rake was defective and that he wanted a brand-new rake. I couldn't believe the nerve of this guy, or that anybody could be that cheap. But ... I just smiled, shook my head and handed him a new nine-dollar rake."

* * *

Charlotte and Tony Dorazio

Tony Dorazio Sr. and his beloved wife, Charlotte (they celebrated their 63rd anniversary on June 15, 2004) sat one late Spring evening at their kitchen table examining pictures of Scotia streets. For each of the photos of the 1940s through 1990s, Tony and Charlotte, it seemed, had a story they could relate to it.

And why not? Tony was born in 1918 on Sacandaga Road, right across the street from their current home and the adjacent family business (Wayside Hardware.) Charlotte was born a few blocks away in a house on Lyric Street.

"We grew up in the same neighborhood. We've known each other forever," Tony said.

The couple was asked if they were childhood or high school sweethearts. Tony, preoccupied with looking at the pictures, did not respond to the question with an answer right away, which prompted some gentle teasing from his wife.

"Hey ... he wants to know if you were my childhood sweetheart!" Charlotte said, repeating the question as she gently shoved his shoulder. Surprised, Tony looked up, laughed and answered, "No, not really. I knew Charlotte and liked her, of course. I used to wave to her when one of us was coming or going. But ... I didn't know what a sweetheart was for a long time. I used to work from 6 a.m. until 11 at night at the (family grocery) store or the farm, and that's no lie."

Some of the Dorazio family's penchant for hard work and honest values dates back to Tony's father, Alexander Dorazio.

"People called him Alec," Dorazio said. "Dad was born in Italy and grew up in an area just southeast of Rome. He first came to this country in 1910. He was astounded by the land that was available here. He always believed that land was the most valuable thing a person can have. Land has value; even back in Italy if you had a little land with a little garden you could work, why then you were well-to-do."

Tony discovered over the years that with long hours and hard work, the land rewards such an owner with opportunity and profit.

In addition to hard work and dedication, another characteristic of the Dorazio family has been constant through the various generations. That characteristic is respect for the customer and fellow citizen.

"I've always thought of it this way -- you don't just sell something to somebody. You tell them what they need, and you show them how to use it," Dorazio said.

Dorazio believes the "Baby Boomers," the generation just after his -- most of whom these days are becoming grandparents -- were and still are a group especially in need of help from stores such as his.

"The older generation of people MY age -- the ones who came back from World War II -- turned out to be a pretty affluent society," he said. "People of my generation made pretty good money, and so they could afford to have someone fix anything that went wrong in the house. The sad part about that, though, is that as a result, those fathers never taught their sons how to work with tools. That meant that many members of that next generation -- the Baby Boomers -- didn't know how to do anything. They would come into the store for advice on how to do some plumbing or carpentry job, and so we'd tell them. We'd always encourage them and say, 'Hey ... you can do this. It's not that hard a job.' The nice part was when they'd come back a few days later and thank us and say, 'You were right. I did it!' "

Tony and Charlotte Dorazio consider themselves lucky to have lived nearly their entire lives in the village of Scotia. Their love for the community is surpassed only by their love for each other and their family.

"Somewhere in the house I even have a big, old key to the front door of the original part of the Glen Sanders Mansion," Tony said with a wide smile. "An old friend of ours used to be the caretaker at the mansion -- you know, back in the 1950s when it was vacant much of the time. He used to take care of the grounds and shut the water off before winter -- that kind of thing."

At the interviewer's request to see the key, Dorazio's smile widened even more.

"Well, as I said, it's somewhere in the house. Years ago, I put it somewhere safe, so I wouldn't lose it. But now I don't know exactly where it is. It's still here ... somewhere."

Wayside Home and Garden Center is still here, too.

Part V
(Baseball) Diamonds are Forever

Growing up in Scotia in the 1950s and 1960s, as I did, offered a wonderful opportunity to watch, play and learn the game of baseball -- the wonderful sport of baseball -- at some of the nicest and well-kept fields and diamonds you could find anywhere.

Some of those fields are still around. Some, alas, are not. From my own perspective, I learned much of the skills and knowledge of the game from my own mother (Ruth, a Brooklyn Dodgers fan), my father (Larry, a New York Yankees fan) and my maternal grandmother (Cecile Brooks, a New York Giants fan.) It was Gram, actually, who taught me how to make up a scoresheet and keep score of a game. I still have some of her old scoresheets, including one she kept of Don Larsen's perfect game in the 1956 World Series.

It was Dad who patiently taught me how to throw, catch and hit a ball. It was with my friends and schoolyard buddies -- Billy Vazal, Al DeCrosta, Russ Hawkins, Grant Downs and others) at the old Mohawk School playground diamond where I played it and played it and played it for hours upon end during the spring, summer and fall months of my youth. It actually was a tiny little field, more like a softball field, with a chain-link right field fence which ran along the Riverside Avenue boundary. This made it a fairly easy home run target if you were a left-handed hitter (which I wasn't), except that there were four or five huge maple trees along the street, and we kids used to have an unofficial ground rule that the ball was still in play if it hit a tree and bounced back on the field, so sometimes you were "robbed" of a homer by a tree trunk or branch.

Mohawk School. That's where I learned how to play. I started out pretty young, and it was a thrill when some of the bigger kids (11, 12 or 13 years old) would have a game and they'd let some of us little guys (7, 8 or 9 years old) play. The big kids, though, would

1959 SCOTIA LL CHAMPS

The Kiwanis team which won the 1959 Scotia Little League championship gathers on the field at Collins Park. First row, from left, are: coach Scott Crowe, Alan Hart, John Wells, Joe Pitts, Don Hogan, Jim Mahoney, Jerry Winkler and manager Don Bovee. Second row, from left: John Van Wormer, Alan DeCrosta, John Krawiecki, Ed Bylina, (unidentified.) Top row, from left: Mike Macejka, Dick Malloy, Larry Ploetz, coach Tony DiCerbo, Bob Malloy and Ed Luberda. (Larry Hart collection.)

always tell me to go way out in deep left field where there was seldom any action, while they'd take all the "good" positions up close. To this day, I think that's why I am primarily an outfielder -- because that's where I first learned to play. (When I got older, I returned the favor, in a way, by letting younger kids play and learn -- just as I had been given that chance.)

Just when I started to think I was getting pretty good at this game of baseball (I knew the starting lineups of EVERY major league team when I was 8) and played make-believe games in my yard hitting "sock" balls around which my mother fashioned out of torn and used socks), along came my first experience with organized baseball. At 10 years old, I tried out for Scotia Little League -- for boys 8 through 12 years old.

Little League, in 1957, was still very much in its infancy in America, including in Scotia where it had only been founded earlier in the decade. I had watched a few games as a younger kid with my dad at the present Little League field site at the southeastern end of Collins Park, and I was eager to try out in April of 1957. It was quite a bit more challenging then, if I may say so, to make it as a Little Leaguer. About 200 kids in Scotia tried out for about 20 open roster spaces. Only the very best made it. Many were cut the first day, others a few days later.

Me? I was all set up for the first real heartbreak of my life. I had survived the first few cuts and was practicing with Rotary, one of the four teams in the circuit at that time. I went to a practice at the main field one evening in early May on the night the manager -- "Tick" Turnbull -- was poised to pass out the uniforms to all the players. I still remember it was a rainy night, and therefore the team was meeting in the upstairs room. There I was, expecting to get my itchy, woolen gray Rotary uniform with the black lettering on it, and I was going to take it home and sleep with it on me. I was so excited!

But wait ... Mr. Turnbull saw me coming in the room. Suddenly, he walked over to me and kind of took me over near the stairs to talk to me privately. He told me, very sadly but in no uncertain teams, that he was sorry but that I was not going to make the team. He could only keep a certain number of boys, and I had almost made it but -- not quite. I was the last kid cut from the team. Mr. Turnbull, while the coaches (Mr. Fellows and Mr. Sykes) were passing out uniforms out of a big box to the other kids, urged me to keep at it and work hard in the weekday morning "farm team" league, which was a loosely organized league of kids playing in street clothes on the softball fields at the park. He said he'd keep an eye on me and he told me to try out again next year as an 11-year-old.

I was crushed. My father, who was waiting for me outside in the car, tried to console me on the way home and told me he'd work with me some more in the backyard and at Mohawk School (which he did!) to get better. At that moment, though, all I could do was cry until my eyes were red. I was so mad at baseball! I swore I would never play it again. This protest lasted less than 24 hours, because next afternoon I was out on the Mohawk School field again, ready to start over.

The story had a happy ending for me. The next spring, I did try out again, and this time I made it -- with a Kiwanis team managed by Mr. Don Bovee. He was a jovial, rotund man with a wide smile. He told me that happy May afternoon that I had made the club and to come to his house at 23 Bruce Street -- sometime over the weekend -- to pick up my uniform.

I was at his door the next morning, and he handed me my

long-awaited scratchy, itchy uniform with KIWANIS in block letters across the front and a big No. 7 on the back -- all in bright red. Then he gave me a red cap with a white triangle in front with the red letter "K" on it.

I wore that cap for the next two years until the white part was smeared brown from dirt and grime. I am certain that I was the proudest Little Leaguer in the village, even though I proved to be one of the league's worst performers of all time. I'm not kidding. I batted .000 as an 11 year old and followed that up with a .080 average the following year in my last go-around. I wasn't a bad outfielder (remember how I played outfield with the big kids at Mohawk School?) but I was, obviously, a bit overmatched at the plate. I DO remember getting an important double to help us win a game in something called the Shaughnessy Cup playoffs, however, so it wasn't a total washout.

When I was 13 I was all set to go on to the next level -- the Babe Ruth League (it had been called the Intermediate League in past years), and I was looking eagerly ahead to playing on the major league-sized diamond (with bases 90 feet apart) at the old layout on Washington Avenue near the railroad tracks. It was a beautiful field surrounded by wooden fences, tucked into a wooded and wild part of the village. (It's gone now and has been replaced by a housing complex.)

If it's true that 13 is an unlucky number, though, then that must be the reason I didn't play as a 13-year-old, after all. In early May of that year, just before Babe Ruth tryouts were to be held, I remember feeling quite sick on a Sunday afternoon. I didn't know what was the matter with me, but all I wanted to do was lie down on a couch. I had no pep; no energy.

Same thing next day. Mom, of course, realized something was up and took me to the doctor. My main physician, Dr. Herman Galster, was away that day but his next-door-neighbor and friend, Dr. Nelson Rust -- the man who had brought me into this world on Nov. 29, 1946 -- told me and my mother what the problem was: it was a bad appendix that had to be removed right away.

So ... there went the baseball season of 1960. No tryout, no fun ... no kidding.

But just like it had been for me in Little League, I was back at it the next year and tried out as a 14-year-old and made, by coincidence, another Kiwanis team -- this time managed by a cigar-smoking, slow-talking but very interesting man named Jim Duncan. He really seemed to like baseball, and he certainly seemed to like managing and advising us kids. I'll tell you another thing I liked about Mr. Duncan -- he was honest and straight with me right from the start, which is not something I can say of too many baseball coaches and managers I have played for over the years, even as an adult. Mr. Duncan told me right up front when he picked me during the tryouts, "You're my extra outfielder and you'll be a guy coming off the bench this year," he said with a hand on my shoulder. "You're not going to play a whole lot. Next year you will, but this year I want you to watch these older guys like (Paul) Schettine and (Tom) Hickey and learn from them how we do things here on Kiwanis."

Duncan was right. I didn't play a whole lot that first year, partly because I broke my right wrist when I slipped and fell on the wet grass during a scrimmage in May. I missed six weeks just when the season was getting started, and when I returned I was pretty rusty. I managed to go 3-for-11 at the plate though, and I was just as proud as anyone else on the squad when we got our championship trophies for winning the league title. It was a championship with which I had very little to do, however. I am being sincere here, not humble.

It's funny how you never recognize the truly defining moments in your life while they are happening; it's only afterward that you look back many years later and say, "Hey ... that was really special."

It was special, because I just assumed that would be one of many championship teams on which I would play the rest of my life. Know what? I've never been on another one since. That was it, back in 1961. No other team I have ever played on -- in Babe

Ruth, high school or as an adult -- has won a championship since my Kiwanis team of 1961. I've been on teams that have come close, but ... no first places.

I just assumed then in 1962, being on a Kiwanis team that still had terrific players like Butch Hurley, Jerry Hesler and John Kruk, that I was going to pick myself up another championship trophy that summer. But I assumed wrong. How could I, an immature 15-year-old, know that simply wishing for success and working hard for it will not guarantee you anything in life ... especially in sports?

In truth, our Kiwanis team was a very good team. But there was a team called Whites (named for sponsor White's Funeral Home) which had a great club with kids like Corky Bleser, Wayne Fetter, Bill Ball, Bob Malloy, John Cottrell and Rick Jurcsak who were determined to knock us off the top. They had a young, smug (it seemed to me at the time) manager named Duane Van Patten, and I took an instant dislike to him and to his whole team. I have always believed that sports teams often take on the character of the coach or manager, and I think this was never more true than it was of Van Patten and the 1962 Whites. They were confident, they had a swagger, they didn't hurt themselves with mistakes and they were very aggressive. They were extremely easy to dislike.

But they were good. They beat us in key games down the stretch, and they won the title.

The mainspring of this Whites team which "stole" our title away, without question, was Bleser. Imagine, if you will, a 15-year-old who at the time was kind of a combination (at the Babe Ruth level) of Derek Jeter, Ty Cobb, Ricky Henderson and Vince Coleman all rolled into one. He could hit, hit with some power, steal bases, field, throw ... and he was smart. Moreover, if you happened to be Bleser's opponent, he was a pain in the neck ... especially so because he wasn't adverse to "talking trash" during a game.

To get an idea of why young Mr. Bleser was so vital to his team, picture this: Bleser, the leadoff hitter, would open a game by walking or getting a single. Then he'd steal second, go to third on a bunt single or a sacrifice bunt by the equally pesty Wayne Fetter, then score on a fly ball or hit by Malloy, Ball or someone else. All in all, Bleser would get on base and then come around to score to make it 1-0 in the total elapsed time of about three minutes. Now, that scenario would be repeated about every two innings every game, so by the sixth inning Whites would be ahead of your team something like 5-1 or 4-2, due in large part to Bleser.

And he played the game hard. Fair, but hard. Once he got on base, he would unnerve the catcher, annoy the pitcher and upset the whole defense before he would inevitably slide hard into the shortstop or second baseman safely with a steal of second. On one such occasion when I was filling in at second for Gary Cole (who was vacationing), Bleser and I had some unfriendly words at second after one of his hard but clean slides ... into me. Even as play was resuming, we were still yapping at each other, daring each other -- until the base umpire behind the mound warned us both to shut up right then or he'd toss both of us out of the game. I zipped it, and so did Bleser. That was probably a good thing for both of us!

Before you go thinking Bleser was the only Babe Ruth opponent I couldn't stomach during games, you're wrong. Every team, it seemed, had at least one guy on it I wished would go 0-for-4 and make five errors every game. On Lions, it was a younger kid named Chris Mabee. He, like Bleser, wasn't lacking in confidence. Unlike Bleser, though, Mabee was a powerful kid with biceps bigger than my thighs! He could hit with tremendous power and, as a right-handed pitcher, he could throw very hard and was just wild enough to keep you very loose in the batter's box.

Anyway, one time that season I led off a Kiwanis game by hitting one of Mabee's fastballs (a nice, fat one right down the middle on the first pitch of the game) right past his head and up the middle to the center fielder on one bounce. It was one of my best hits of the season. When I got to first safely, Mabee muttered something over at me like "Lucky hit" or something, and I chirped back at him about how next time I'd be hitting it off his forehead or something like that, and once again I was in trouble with the base umpire. I have never in my life been thrown out of a game by an umpire, but I think I came pretty close in those two games with Bleser and Mabee.

So ... the season gradually wound down. After the season had started out in such promising fashion from both a team and personal standpoint, it all unraveled for both Kiwanis and Alan Hart in August. I went into the worst slump of my life. I went something like 0-for-18 or 0-for-20 over the last four or five games and we just lost, lost, lost. And Whites won the title. For many months afterward -- well into the winter, in fact -- I felt like I had let myself down, as well as everyone on the team. I felt it was my fault that we had lost. After all, I had dropped from well over .300 in early July down to .222 at the end of the season. Ouch!

Then something happened the following March which changed my whole life and my whole personality, in a very real sense. I went out for the Scotia High baseball tryouts and quickly discovered that not only did I still love baseball but that I had two great teammates to play alongside. Their names were Corky Bleser and Chris Mabee!

When practice began in the high school gym, I saw both those old antagonists holding their gloves with all the rest of the guys trying out and I thought, "Aw, great. These two SOBS are on the team too. This is really going to be a long season." As it turned out, it was a wonderful season.

Many years later, when I was a sports writer for the *Times Union*, I interviewed Jon Mueller -- a fellow whom I had watched grow from a terrific high school athlete at Stillwater High to the point where he became a tremendous professional baseball player with the Albany Diamond Dogs. Mueller, who is now the baseball coach at University at Albany, told me during that interview that one thing which playing baseball, basketball and football had taught him was that in sports, often your worst enemy can become your best friend.

Looking back now on my life, I know Mueller was correct, because Bleser and Mabee became not only my teammates but good friends -- once we were wearing the same uniform in 1963 and 1964. Bleser broke the ice for both of us in spring practices one day by giving me the nickname of "Jap," in reference to the fact that I wore a blue velvet jacket adorned with silver dragons and yellow suns which my Uncle Bob Hart had brought back from the Orient during his hitch in the U.S. Navy.

The nickname stuck for that whole spring, and I liked it, and I soon realized -- thank goodness -- that a kid I once couldn't stand when I was playing against him was really a darn good guy when he was on your team. So was Mabee, who was still throwing nasty fastballs and hitting towering homers but now suddenly was a lot of fun to be around --especially sitting next to him when he was making wisecracks on a bus ride to or from a game. (Bleser, Dave Smith and Hesler were also great at this.)

Playing high school ball was different from Babe Ruth baseball in many ways. It was a much shorter season, and it all seemed to mean more. It was more public, because all the results and linescores were recorded in the newspapers, and also there was kind of an enlarged sense of purpose somehow because you were representing not only your team but your school. (I guess that's the whole point?)

In my junior year (1963) I was on the JV club, which played its home games at Collins Park on the legendary diamond by the lake. It was a blast to play there, and our JV team was a good one. We seldom lost, and sometimes we won by lopsided scores. I had a pretty good pitching record that year, something like 5-0 (I was strictly a pitcher then), because I was supported by a ton of runs each game. I did have one tremendous JV game I'll always remember though -- a one-hit shutout against old St. Mary's of Amsterdam down on that Collins Park diamond.

The following year, my senior year of 1964, was a different story. I made the varsity, but I didn't see a lot of action early in the year, simply because we had an awesome team with a staff of pitchers much better than I was. We had Mabee and Hesler as our main starters, and they did most of our pitching. Once in awhile guys like me, Tom Onderchain or someone else would come in in relief. I DID manage to cost us a game at Mont Pleasant in one of our first games of the year. I threw one pitch -- a mushball curve that got too much of the plate -- in the seventh inning with the bases loaded and gave up a screaming, game-winning hit to a guy named Jack Laflin. I then got one start early in the year at Mohonasen and got knocked out early, giving up a home run and putting us in a 4-0 hole after two innings. We came back and tied it at 4, but we still eventually lost, 5-4.

Remember me saying earlier how you don't recognize the important, defining moments in your life as they happen? Here's another one of mine: It occurred right about the middle of May of that senior year. Several members of the team decided to quit the baseball team, for various reasons. To be perfectly honest, I thought once or twice about quitting, too. I was discouraged that I wasn't playing very often, and I was screwing up pretty royally when I was playing. I was pretty low in spirits. But I decided I owed it to my teammates -- guys like Bleser and Mabee, who I had come to like enormously as friends -- not to let them down and at least stick it out and support them while sitting on the bench or throwing in the bullpen.

Boy, am I glad I stayed with it! With Hesler and Mabee working many innings a week because of makeups of postponements, there suddenly was a lot of work for me and anyone else who could pitch as the season wore to its finish. Suddenly, too, with all the easy throwing I had been doing in the bullpen every game and every practice just for something to do, my arm seemed to get as strong as it ever had been or has ever been since. I felt good and strong, and I was throwing harder than I ever had, and the ball inexplicably was going wherever I wanted to throw it.

I had a couple of good relief outings in late May and, to my surprise, Mr. Ellithorpe said to me one evening just as practice was ending, "Be ready to pitch tomorrow, Alan. You're starting -- here at home against Mohonasen."

Wow. It just didn't get any better than that. A start, on the home field behind the high school ... with home fans, friends and family watching. A chance to atone for that poor start against that same Mohonasen team.

It was May 26th, 1964, and it was a classic warm, dry late May afternoon with a light breeze blowing in from the West from behind the U.S. Navy Depot buildings beyond the left field fence.

I'll never forget the day if I live to be 102. My mound opponent was Bruce Wheeler, the Mighty Warriors' classy all-around athlete. Little did I know what was going to happen in the next three hours or so.

Both teams settled into a tight game, and after seven innings (regulation for high school) both starting pitchers -- myself and Wheeler -- were still in there and it was tied at 1. (It's not that I was overpowering as a pitcher, mind you; I had great defense in back of me. There were many grounders hit to the left side of the infield, and Bleser (shortstop) and Fetter (third base) were just like vaccuum cleaners fielding everything hit to them. Finally, as it was getting pretty dark and hard to see, I managed to get Mohonasen out in the top of the ninth (the second extra inning), and the home-plate umpire told both managers that this bottom half of the ninth was going to be "it." Either we would score and win the game, or it would end up in a tie, because it was getting too dark to see.

Well, Wayne Fetter walked and stole second to lead off the inning, and I was getting pretty excited that I might finally be a winning pitcher -- after all -- in a varsity high school game. But suddenly there was one out, then two, and Fetter was still on second. It looked for the world like the game would end in a tie. The only person standing in Wheeler's way of salvaging a tie for his team was a kid named Ralph Stevens. Ralphie was a big, friendly kid who was a left-handed hitter and a pretty darn good one. What happened? Stevens, who is probably known more for having been a reliable shooter and rebounder in basketball than for his baseball exploits, lined a sharp single right through the box and on into center field. Fetter, probably the fastest runner on our team, scored standing up and we won, 2-1. That hit made me the happiest 17-year-old in America right about that moment, and I ran out and jumped on Stevens like Yogi Berra hugging Don Larsen in October of '56.

It was the one and only high school pitching victory I ever got, as it turned out. Had I quit two or three weeks earlier, obviously, it never would have happened. I got a very stark, vivid reminder of a valuable life lesson right there -- don't quit on yourself or others. Hang in there when things get tough, if only for the sake of others with whom you have made a commitment.

It was all over a few days later. We had tied for the last playoff spot in the Section II tournament, and we had to play Saratoga High in an outbracket game at Burnt Hills on Memorial Day morning for the right to go in the tournament. We played 17 innings, and we lost. I remember pitching from the 10th through the 16th innings, and leaving a terrible mess (bases loaded, no outs) for poor teammate Tom Onderchain to have to clean up. Clean it up he did, though, with a couple of strikeouts and an infield popup. Then we

Hart Stops Mohonasen In 2-1 Duel

Righthander Alan Hart outdueled Mohonasen's Bruce Wheeler to give Scotia High a 2-1, nine-inning victory over the Warriors yesterday in a non-league baseball meeting at Scotia.

Hart, who scattered seven hits in a strong mound performance, also tallied the deciding run in the bottom of the second extra inning on Ralph Stevens' single. Hart had walked to open the inning, was scrificed to second and moved to third after a fly ball. Wheeler allowed five hits.

Wayne Fetter walked, stole second and tallied on Johnny Kruk's double for the first Scotia run in the initial frame. Mohonasen tied it up at 1-1 in the fourth on Jim Krone's single and Dan Lucca's double.

The victory lifted the Scotia record to 10-6 with a home test against Mont Pleasant on tap today. Line score:

Mohonasen 000 100 000—1 7 1
Scotaia ... 100 000 001—2 5 2
  Wheeler and Serapilio; Hart and Bowers.

This Schenectady Gazette newspaper clipping of May 27, 1964, is one of the author's most valued possessions as it reflects one of the happiest days of his young life: the only varsity pitching victory of his life! The clipping, unfortunately, does not point out the great infield defense that day behind Hart -- mostly by shortstop Corky Bleser and third baseman Wayne Fetter. Also, the second paragraph of the article is incorrect. Wayne Fetter, not Hart, walked and scored the winning run.

lost the next inning. The season, and my humble but enjoyable high school sports career as a player, was over.

Is baseball a great game, or what? The whole baseball experience of playing sandlot, Little League, Babe Ruth and Scotia High baseball taught me so many things about life. It is the nature of sports to do exactly that -- to drive us to find not only the best that is within us individually but to also to learn to work together and get along with other people, teammates and oppponents alike, and to lift each other up.

I know this: some of the best friends I have ever had in this world I met through sports, and I know I am not alone in that.

* * *

Fred "Corky" Bleser

Frederick Jacob Bleser Jr., better known throughout Scotia the last half of the 20th century as "Corky" Bleser, winced and then smiled widely when reminded how about 40 years earlier he once had dubbed a certain teammate with the nickname of "Jap" because of a bright, Asian-looking jacket the teammate wore.

"Did I start that? I remember the coat, but I don't remember giving you the nickname," Bleser said as he settled in for a long chat with this writer over cups of coffee at the Glenville Queen diner one rain-soaked May afternoon. "It sounds like me, though. I was always talking too much, even during games. I used to get guys on other teams mad because I played hard and I talked a lot. For me, though, it was just between the lines and when the game was over, it was over. Then I'd see those same guys like Bill Martin and Mike Macejka afterward, and those guys you'd been competing so hard against were your friends and it was all forgotten."

Bleser, unquestionably, in his youth was one of the best teen-aged athletes in the village of Scotia's history. He was the point guard of the 1963-64 Scotia High varsity basketball team which won the Section II Class A title. He was the starting shortstop on the varsity baseball team for two years and one of its best hitters.

81

Scotia High's varsity baseball team in 1964 finished its season by losing a 17-inning marathon sectional game to Saratoga in a game played at neutral Burnt Hills. Seated in first row, from left, are: Joe Palma, Corky Bleser, John Kruk, Alan Hart, Chris Mabee, Dave Smith and Wayne Fetter. Standing, from left: manager Tom Castner, Don Bowers, Jerry Hesler, Larry Ploetz, Ralph Stevens, John Cottrell, Tom Onderchain, Dave Wagner and coach Cecil "Pete" Ellithorpe. (Scotia High yearbook photo, 1965.)

And whereas "Jap" was a nickname which only stuck with this author for about two months, "Corky" is a nickname by which Bleser has been known -- and one he has embraced -- virtually his entire 57 years.

"My (paternal) grandmother was responsible for it," Bleser explained. "My grandfather's name was Jake, and my father was Frederick Jacob, so they used to call my grandfather Big Jake and my father Little Jake. I was born Frederick Jacob Jr., and right away my grandmother told my mom and dad, 'Hey, we're not going to go through this Big Jake and Little Jake thing again. You're going to have to call this little guy something else.' Well, there was an athlete at Mont Pleasant right around then named Corky Stanton, and that's where Dad got the name Corky. I've always liked it. When I went in the service (U.S. Air Force) I went away from it, but once I came home, I went back to it because that's how everybody I know here knows me."

Anyone who went to school with Bleser, or had the experience of playing sports with or against him, cannot forget the name or the athlete. He was the ultimate competitor, the consummate teammate.

"Dad had a lot to do with instilling in me an interest in sports," Bleser said fondly of his father, who died in 1991. (A sad note: Bleser's mother, Emily, died in the spring of 2004, 11 days after this interview.) "Dad never missed any of my games. He was always there. And he kept a scrapbook of the things I did."

It's a hefty scrapbook of clippings, chronicling an impressive youth in which Bleser was a standout in baseball (Little League, Babe Ruth and high school) and high school basketball.

These days, if Bleser chooses to get the scrapbook off the shelf, he has plenty of accomplishments to show the many family members who make up his support system. Bleser, who has been a line foreman for Niagara Mohawk (Schenectady office) for 34 years, has been married to the former Kathy Sweet since 1970. They have three children -- Amy, Kate and Mark. Mark is currently a junior at Johnson and Wales, R.I., where he is captain of the soccer team.

He did not play a fall sport in his later years, but if he had it's likely he would have been the school's best cross country runner or best soccer player or top football player.

In the spring, though, Bleser was ready with his glove and bat. He played with a passion and an obvious deep respect for the game.

Had Corky Bleser chosen to go out for soccer in his own high school days, who knows? He might have excelled in that sport, too. (The sport was introduced in the fall of 1963 -- Bleser's junior year.)

Bleser smiled and shrugged at the suggestion.

"I played a little football in the fall when I started high school, but I got a concussion and got some headaches from it, so I just got away from it and concentrated on baseball and basketball," he explained. "I liked them both -- baseball and basketball -- but as I got older, I have to say I liked basketball the most."

Bleser played baseball, however, as though he loved it.

"I was lucky," he said as his mind raced back to his Little League days of the mid-1950s. "I was drafted right away when I was 8 by Rotary manager Tick Turnbull, so I got to play for him for five years. I got the chance to learn from kids like Dennis Gregorie, Doug Sykes and Ricky Berger as I grew up on the team."

Bleser learned his lessons fast ... and well. He was a catcher and infielder for Rotary, and made the All-Star team. He considers his most memorable LL game the day he caught Mike Macejka's no-hitter at the Schenectady Little League field in the District 12 All-Star Tournament.

"Tick Turnbull was a great manager and coach. He taught me a lot, not just about how to play ball but also how to prepare yourself for sports each day. He ran things his way, and we had a good team. You learned from him not to swim, run or overdo the day of a game so you could conserve your energy."

Then came the Babe Ruth years with Whites and manager Duane Van Patten. Bleser loved that chapter of his life when he wore the gray and green of Whites from 1960 through 1962.

"He was a player's coach," he said of Van Patten. "He could relate to kids our age because he was pretty young himself, just starting a family. He was a weight lifter, and he was amazingly strong. When I tried out at age 13, he got behind me one time and picked me up with one hand and lifted me up over his head and back down -- with one hand! Now, I only weighed 100 pounds or something back then, but ... wow!"

That word of "Wow!" could sum up the impact which Bleser himself had on the Whites championship club of 1962, and on the Scotia High varsities of 1964 and 1965. He was a gifted hitter who could work a count, hit the ball where it was pitched with a hard, level swing and get on base. Once on base, he was nearly unstoppable.

There was more: he was a cerebral player, too. He could pick up opposing team's signs. He didn't make mistakes on the basepaths, and he didn't make poor decisions with what to do with the ball if it were hit to him.

"That whole summer, there was one team (Kiwanis) where the manager (Jim Duncan) would kick the dirt in the third base coaching box if he wanted someone to steal. We always knew what was coming, so we usually threw the guy out," Bleser smiled. "On Whites, we didn't have any team signs. We were on our own. When I was going to try to steal, I had my own private sign that I had with Wayne Fetter, who was up after me. If I was going to go, I'd give Wayne some signal that I was going to go, and then it was up to him whether he wanted to swing at it or not. The other teams didn't pick up on it."

Bleser's baseball talent, energy and resourcefulness were put to ample use in high school, too. Many a youth baseball coach or manager, since the game began, has chosen to put his best defensive player at shortstop. That's the position Bleser patrolled for the late Pete Ellithorpe's Scotia High varsity as a junior and senior.

"I loved playing high school ball," Bleser said. "Like with Rotary and Whites ... it was special. We all seemed to enjoy being on the team. Those long bus rides to and from places like Johnstown and Gloversville ... with guys like Chris Mabee and Dave Smith making jokes. Who can forget that?"

Who indeed? And who, if he ever played against him or alongside him, can ever forget Corky Bleser?

Bill Vazal, a teammate of Bleser's on the 1960 and 1961 Whites teams, and also on the Scotia High baseball teams of 1964 and 1965, has nothing but fond memories of being a teammate of Bleser's. Like Bleser, Vazal enjoyed the experience of playing Babe Ruth ball for Whites and the young manager, Van Patten.

"He was a fascinating guy, and just a great guy to play for," Vazal recalled. "I remember one night we were playing on that old ballfield on Washington Avenue and a bad storm suddenly came up. Turned out it was a tornado in some parts of the area. Well, both teams got in the dugouts and we waited it out for awhile. After a few minutes, Van -- we called him Van -- said to us, 'OK fellas, we've all got metal cleats on. Let's all hold hands and go out there on the field. If one of us goes, we all go!' He was only joking, of course. It cracked us up.' "

Part VI
What a Sight (Site?) to See!

When you grow up in a village such as Scotia, I guess when you are a kid you tend to take most things for granted ... especially things like old buildings.

Young children and teen-agers and, sadly, some adults, don't have any appreciation for buildings that have been around a long time. I used to be that way ... until I was about 18 or 20 years old. I'd think, "Hey, that building is OLD! Get rid of it. Knock it down. Build something new."

At some point in my life, though, I did a 180-degree turn. I think it was around 1966, 1967 when some people in town (politicians and businessmen) were talking about the need to demolish the Glen Sanders Mansion and put a new business there. Or a parking lot.

Thanks in large part to my dear, late father Larry Hart, however, that never happened.

My father, who was Schenectady's city and county historian for many years with a lifelong appreciation for things historic, went to war with these people who were bent on putting a wrecking ball to the Glen Sanders Mansion, and I was very, very proud of Dad for helping these people come to their senses. It's a fact that my father had a great deal to do with the saving of the Sanders Mansion. He wrote heartfelt columns about it in *The Daily Gazette*, where he was a reporter and columnist from 1960 until 1999. He went to board meetings and council meeings and just generally told many a politico to their face that if they were really serious about tearing down the Glen Sanders Mansion, they were myopic, stupid or both and that they ought to be ashamed of themselves. I agreed wholeheartedly with my father on this, because -- like many people in Scotia -- I loved the Sanders Mansion, too. I still do. I used to walk and ride past it on my bicycle as a kid and a teen, and also drove past it in my car as an older teen. I had tours through the building in my grade school days. It would have been a shame to lose such an important part of our village's and nation's history.

Fortunately, the mansion survived. After Dad helped see to it that the wrecking ball never got near the place, the building and grounds were purchased by Dr. and Mrs. Dolph G. Ebeling , who "moved into the mansion in the early 1970s and made extensive renovations and repairs," according to my father in his 1988 book, "Schenectady: Changing with the Times."

The original mansion (there were two, actually) was built by Alexander Lindsey Glen in 1658. Lindsey, who was born in Inverness, Scotland in 1610, took the surname Glen from the Glen Estk in Scotland when he came here to this country in 1643 as an agent for the Dutch East India Company.

When the Schenectady stockade was raided and burned by the French and Indians in February of 1690, John Alexander Glen (Alexander Lindsey Glen's son) was living in the mansion and was known by the French as a friend to all. So Glen and his family and friends, plus some who had fled the Stockade and escaped the carnage there, were spared.

The mansion was rebuilt in 1713, mostly from the same materials of the original mansion. At that time Jacob (John Alexander's son), owned it and was living there. He only had one child, a daughter named Debora. She married John Sanders of Albany in 1739, so the home finally took the name of Glen Sanders Mansion.

Some of the factual information above I derived from writings of my father, and some from a booklet entitled "Scotia," co-authored by Scotians William M. Nicoll and W. Stewart Cole. It was published in 1914 by The Citizen Publishing Company of Schenectady. The booklet had this to say about the Glen Sanders Mansion and the families who lived there:

"During these trying days of our American Revolution from 1776 to 1783, this Scotia house again was the cause of relief to the inhabitants of Schenectady, for by reason of the great

These photographs show various views of the Glen Sanders Mansion as it looked in 1952. The building, which still stands as part of a luxurious inn/restaurant complex at the eastern end of the village on the banks of the Mlohawk River, originally was built in 1658 by Alexander Lindsey Glen. It was rebuilt out of many of the same materials in 1713 by Jacob Glen. (Larry Hart collection.)

friendship existing between the families of Sir William Johnson and the Glens, the bloody raids of Schoharie and Cherry Valley were made by going around by South to avoid their friends in Schenectady."

As we all know now, the building persevered -- in large part thanks to my father. It is now a thriving restaurant/inn (owned by Angelo Mazzone) and one of the most popular entertainment spots in the Capital Region. Improvements and annexations to the building have resulted in quite a different look to the site from what it looked like when I was growing up in the 1950s and 1960s. From an aesthetic and historical standpoint, I think that the "modernization" of the Glen Sanders Mansion is unfortunate. I wish instead that it had been left in its original state -- as it looked from 1713 on into the 1990s. But ... at least the mansion has been preserved in some state instead of being torn down. We can be grateful at least for that much.

The Glen Sanders Mansion is not the only beautiful, old building people or historic or noteworthy spot which people who call Scotia their hometown think of when conversation turns to familiar places.

Here are a few more which come to mind right away:

41 SACANDAGA ROAD

This beautiful old home on Sacandaga Road used to be "at the outskirts of town." Now, it's right in the center.

"I remember the Layton family used to live there," said Joan (Spencer) Szablewski, current Town of Glenville historian. "My family lived across the street when I was a child. They used to have a lush, green lawn that they manicured to perfection and they told all of us kids to stay off of it. So, of course, we all made it a point to go out and step on it and play on it all we could. An old woman named Edith Whitbeck lived there a long time, too."

Before that, Szablewski also lived on Pershing Drive during her childhood. She remembers something during that time that young people of today probably cannot fathom: a visit from the

The home at 41 Sacandaga Road was once considered on the outskirts of town. In the early photo (top) taken in 1904, a little girl named Edith Whitbeck in identifiable in the surrey. The bottom photo shows how the house looked 83 years later in November of 1987. (Larry Hart collection.)

ice man. This was in the days before refrigerators and freezers. Homeowners had something called an "ice box," and a block of ice was placed in it to keep food fresh.

"I was 11 or 12 years old, and we didn't have a refrigerator yet," Szablewski said. "I remember the ice man coming to the house with our block of ice."

Ruth (Brooks) Hart (the author's mother) remembers similar visits.

"It sounds kind of messy, but it wasn't," Hart said. "What you did was put a pan under the ice box to catch any water that would drip down as the ice melted. But we didn't have that problem in the summertime at our house, because our dog used to go under there and drink up the cold water. He used to lie under there, too, to keep cool when it was hot."

THE SCOTIA FIREHOUSE

Next to the Glen Sanders Mansion, the fire station is probably the most recognizable structure in town. It's a reference point for directions (How often have you told someone, for example, "The bowling alley? Why, it's on Mohawk Avenue on the left-hand side -- first light past the firehouse.") It's been around since before the automobile, and it's right in the middle of the village.

The fire station -- as this book is being written in 2004 -- is a controversial subject in the village. Also the home to the village's police department (Ten Broeck Street entrance), the building is inadequate and old. A proposal to build a new fire station (on Glen Avenue and Ballston Avenue) was soundly defeated in April of 2004.

The Scotia Fire Department was formed in November of 1873 and at the time was called The Neptune Engine Company of Scotia. The company had two hand engines -- Neptune No. 4 (which the village bought from ALCO in Schenectady) and Neptune No. 6 (which the village purchased from Union College.)

The Scotia Fire Department has had the corner of Mohawk Avenue and Ten Broeck Street as its location for well over a century. In the above photos of 1890 and 1917 (note the Red Cross flag above the entrance) horses are ready and waiting if called. In the photo below (circa 1985), department captain Jim Campbell stands alongside one of the engines. (Larry Hart collection.)

Time for a joke: A horse walks into a bar. The bartender looks up at the horse and says, "Hey Buddy, why the long face?" (People always wait for a punch line here, but ... that's the whole joke, because horses all have long faces. Get it? Yeah, I know ... it's pretty lame. But I like it!)

Anyway, retired Scotia fire chief Al Falcon told me a story one day that has been handed down over the generations of firemen who have served at the firehouse on Mohawk Avenue. It seems the establishment right across the street on the south side of Mohawk Avenue has always been a restaurant/grill as far back as anyone can remember, just as it is at this writing (it's called O'Leary's now.) Well, according to Falcon, one day one of the horses belonging to the fire company was being washed or groomed or something, and when the handler looked away for a second, the horse walked right across Mohawk Avenue and under the trees, and -- to the amazement of patrons in the tavern there -- walked right up to the front door of the bar! (Maybe that was how the horse/bar jokes got started?)

One thing which Scotians learn very quickly about the fire station is to try never to be close to it at noontime or when a fire is announced, because that noon whistle (more like an ocean liner's warning!) will lift you right out of your laced-up sneakers with the noise. It is deafening.

Funny, though: some people say you get used to it.

"I lived on James Street in back of the Baptist church for my first 24 years," said Sharon (Hartley) Dunlap. "The whistle? After awhile, it got so I didn't even really notice it."

Speaking of whistles, here are a couple more memories: from Ruth (Brooks) Hart, and Mary (Sturdy) Kelefant, who is the author's mother-in-law. Both women have memories of the firehouse from their respective teen years during the late 1930s, but the memories have nothing to do with the building's whistle. Rather, the memories have everything to do with the whistles of the firemen themselves.

"I never liked walking past that corner," Ruth Hart recalled.

"The men would sit outside and whistle and hoot at us girls whenever we went by. I didn't care for that."

But Mary Kelefant smiles now at mention of this time-honored tradition (also common at construction sites) of men whistling at pretty lasses.

"That sort of thing never bothered me," she said. "They used to sit on their lawn chairs outside the firehouse on Mohawk Avenue on sunny days, getting their sun tans. We used to call them 'Sunfish.' "

SCOTIA COMMONS

The building on Mohawk Avenue now known as Scotia Commons is the site of several businesses. It once served as the official town hall for the Town of Glenville before the town offices moved to the current location on Glenridge Road.

Many people who were once teen-agers in Scotia during the 1960s and can remember going to dances in that building might be surprised to learn that there are people who sincerely believe that the building is currently haunted by a ghost -- a female ghost, to be specific about it.

Sharon (Hartley) Dunlap

Sharon (Hartley) Dunlap worked at a business firm at Scotia Commons for 11 years until the spring of 2004. Dunlap knows about the apparition; she has not seen it with her own eyes, but has felt its presence.

"I haven't seen it, but I've known it's been around," Dunlap said. "Strange things have happened; drawers would open and close, Venetian blinds would roll up and down by themselves. One morning I got there at 6:30 and was getting the coffee going, and I heard beeping noises that ordinarily tell you someone else is in the building. I thought it was a co-worker friend, Paul, and I yelled to him, 'Hi, Paul -- I'm in here.' But ... there was no one else in the building."

Dunlap said others in the building have similar and even more vivid stories about the Scotia Commons Ghost.

"Up in the old gym, one of the ladies saw the ghost one day. She said it was a woman in Victorian dress -- very colorful clothing," Dunlap said. "And one of the guys I worked with saw it from the waist up and is sure it was a woman. Another lady who worked there heard a piano playing there once when she was all alone. Well, there's only one piano in the building and it has broken keys!"

Want more?

"Another lady was working there alone in the building one evening this past winter," Dunlap said. "She started hearing noises, and finally, she was aware of something standing behind her, and she said she felt her hair stand up on the back of her neck. Then she heard hissing behind her, so she quickly gathered up her stuff and left. She figured the ghost didn't want her around and was telling her to leave. She left!"

THE POST OFFICE

Another of Scotia's most recognizable structures of long standing is the U.S. Post Office at 224 Mohawk Avenue -- erected in 1940 between tiny Center Street and Sacandaga Road.

One familiar wrinkle to the post office, for any who lived in Scotia during the last half of the 20th century, has to be the compelling mural painting on the East wall of the building. Myself, I remember as a tot going in that building and gazing in awe up at that painting high above me on the wall as we waited in line to be served to send Christmas packages to California. It is a most impressive work, showing detail and imagination as it attempts to depict the contentious meeting between the French and Indians and the Glen family and friends and servants in front of the Sanders mansion on the morning after the Schenectady Stockade was burned and most of its inhabitants slaughtered or taken prisoner on a February night in 1690. The

Here is Scotia's original U.S. Post Office, located at 109 Mohawk Avenue. (Year unknown. Larry Hart collection.)

An empty lot and a home stood on the property of Mohawk Avenue and Center Street (top photo) before the current U.S. Post Office was constructed there in 1940. (Larry Hart collection.)

painting, which is 12 feet wide and five feet high, is called "The Glens Spared by French and Indians, 1690," and it has hung on that wall since Aug. 18, 1941.

I had always assumed the work was painted directly on the smooth cement wall, and I had also assumed that it had been done by a talented Scotia High student or an area painter. My assumptions, as I discovered when I began researching for this book, were both wrong.

"It's painted onto a canvas, and it was hung up there in 1941," a Scotia postal employee (who preferred not to be identified) told me. "I understand there are only 13 like it left in the country, and when this building is torn down someday, that painting is going to be sent to the Smithsonian in Washington (D.C.) as a piece of historic American art."

With good reason. The work, according to a newspaper article in the files of Town of Glenville historian Joan (Spencer) Szablewski, is an "egg tempera" mural and it was painted by one Amy Jones (Mrs. D. Blair Jones) of Saranac Lake. Jones was

A true work of art is available for all to see on the east wall of the Scotia Post Office on Mohawk Avenue. The painting was completed by Amy Jones of Saranac Lake in 1941 and has hung there ever since. (Alan Hart photo.)

99

commissioned by the Federal government to do the work as one of President Franklin D. Roosevelt's New Deal initiatives to put thousands of national artists to work and at the same time promote pride in communities during the Great Depression.

It's a haunting painting, what with the strained looks on the faces of the Glen family and friends on the left and the supposedly peaceful salute of the French officer on the right, plus the Stockade aflame in the background across the frozen Mohawk River. If you've never seen it, or haven't seen it in awhile, go check it out. OK?

THE LIBRARY

To most of us, the old, white-painted building at Collins Park at the corner of Mohawk Avenue and Collins Streets -- built in 1728 -- has always been the Scotia Public Library. It hasn't always been so.

To be precise, it is called the Abraham Glen House. Abraham Glen, the ninth child of John A. Glen, was born in 1694. The home (as well as all the land which is now referred to as Collins Park) became the property of the Collins brothers -- Charles and James -- of Kilrea, Ireland, when they bought it from Theodore W. Sanders in 1842.

The last person to live in the entire house was Miss Annie E. Collins, daughter of Charles. She lived there until her death in 1922. Six years later, the house and the land that is now Collins Park was deeded to the Village of Scotia. (More on this in a chapter to come.)

The above information is from former Scotia historian Donald A. Keefer in an article published in the Scotia *Journal's* Special BiCentennial Section on July 21, 1976. Keefer said of Miss Collins, "The garden and lawns surrounding the old building have been for many years a center of attraction. In her lifetime, Miss Collins spent many hours each day in her gardens. She was a lover of flowers and was singularly succesful in their

The Abraham Glen House, which has served for many years as Scotia's public library, is one of the main attractions of Collins Park. The photograph was taken in November of 1987. (Larry Hart collection.)

cultivation. It is said she had the first tulips of spring and the last flower of fall."

VEEDER'S FORT

Scotia once had its own military fort.

Really. Well, sort of.

In the cemetery area of the lawn in front of the First Reformed Church which overlooks Collins Lake, one will find a prominent headstone in that burial ground -- the stone marking the final resting place of Revolutionary War veteran Nicholas G. Veeder.

Veeder, born on Christmas day in 1760, served with General Nicholas Herkimer and fought in the bloody Battle of Oriskany. After the war, Veeder settled in Scotia. He married an English girl -- Ann Hetherington. They bought a plot of land in the northwest section of the village -- a 124-acre plot that included a humble structure which, according to Larry Hart's "Rambling Through Glenville" column in the Scotia *Journal* of March 10, 1988, was "a queer-looking building that was said to have been an early outpost of the Schenectady Fort in the French and Indian War years."

Veeder and his wife and their two sons, Garrett and Abram, settled on the property. After Veeder became a widower, Garrett also died (from complications of being struck in the eye with the tip of an umbrella during an argument), Nicholas and his surviving son Abram lived at the fort.

"From that time on (Garrett's death), the farm became neglected and gradually was sold off by the 1800s -- except for the fort," according to the Larry Hart column of 1988. "Nicholas Veeder was often asked to serve as parade marshall for Schenectady's July 4th parade. For many years, two men on the city committee were designated to cross the old covered bridge to Scotia, go up to Veeder's fort and bathe him gingerly before he put on his Continental Army uniform. Then he'd be driven back

The old Veeder "Fort" stood near what now is Vley Road and Halcyon Street as part of a 124-acre farm from the early 1700s until it was demolished late in the 19th century. The curious "fort" was the dwelling of Abram Veeder (with top hat) and his father, Revolutionary War veteran Nicholas Veeder. Nicholas lived to be 101; his tombstone may be found in the cemetery of the First Reformed Church on Collins Street. Abram died in 1891 when he was hit by a moving train while walking along the tracks near the fort. (Larry Hart collection.)

across the bridge to the city and given the honor of riding in the lead carriage, bedecked with bunting, on the Fourth of July parade up State Street."

Nicholas Veeder died on April 7, 1862 at age 101. Veeder's tombstone at the Reformed church, by the way, states incorrectly that at his death he was New York State's last surviving veteran of the Revolutionary War. To be exact, he was the last surviving veteran of that war from Schenectady County.

Abram Veeder, meanwhile, apparently was a learned but eccentric individual. He taught school and wore dimes and quarters on his coat in place of buttons. Abram also put the fort (in which he continued to live) to good use. He collected firearms and trinkets which he showed to visitors who came to the fort.

The fort, which had become a magnet for hoboes and drunkards, became something of an eyesore and nuisance to Scotia neighbors by the 1880s. When Abram died in 1891 (he stumbled and fell into a moving train while walking along the tracks near the fort), the fort was soon demolished. A house was built on the site at the corner of Vley Road and Halcyon Street.

Here's a view of Mohawk Avenue looking east from Ballston Avenue in the winter of 1926. (Larry Hart collection.)

The trolley moves along the track at Mohawk Avenue in this photo taken looking east toward the corner of Mohawk and Toll Street in 1916. (Larry Hart collection.)

These businesses were in evidence in 1946 along the north side of Mohawk Avenue east of Ballston Avenue. (Larry Hart collection.)

107

This photograph, taken in 1892, is one of the earliest-known photos of Scotia. The shot, taken from the area that is now Sanders Avenue and Riverside Avenue, shows the First Baptist Church on Mohawk Avenue and the old Mohawk Avenue School (later an ice cream factory) to its left. (Larry Hart collection.)

The village of Scotia has long been a haven for bowling enthusiasts. The Scotia Bowling Palace, shown in this early photo (circa 1939), is still where keglers go to meet and socialize these days, but the Mohawk Avenue establishment is now known as Rolling Greens Lanes. (Larry Hart collection and Alan Hart photo.)

Scotia's main street, Mohawk Avenue, as it appeared when looking west at the junction of Ballston Avenue in 1954. (Larry Hart collection.)

Part VII
I'm "Walkin'," Yes Indeed!

I am a very lucky man. Not only am I happily married, but I have a wonderful mother-in-law. Her name is Mary (Sturdy) Kelefant, and she is 81 years old and has lived in Scotia virtually her entire life.

Mary's childhood and teen years were spent growing up in a house at 203 Glen Avenue, a block south of the fire station on Mohawk Avenue and a block north of Mohawk School on Sanders Avenue. For over 50 years, she has lived on the corner of Albermarle Road and Neal Street -- a stone's toss from the high school.

Mary (Sturdy) Kelefant

Those crude "mother-in-law" jokes are not applicable with Mary, whom I have been most privileged for the past 10 years to call "Mom." (I married her daughter, the former Mary Carol Kelefant/Westad on May 22, 1994.) Mom Kelefant is a great friend and a fine person.

On top of these attributes, I can now tell you this about Mary Kelefant: she is a tremendous resource on Scotia history. I noticed early in my whirlwind courtship of her daughter that Mom Kelefant seemed to be a walking, talking encyclopedia of history on Scotia. She always seemed to know who used to live in this house or that house, who was married to whom and how many children they had and all their kids' names. She also used to describe the interiors of many of the houses in town, saying something like, "Oh, I remember the Martins. They lived on (Such-and-such) Avenue and they had a big kitchen in the back of the house that looked out on Sacandaga Road. And they had one of the first air conditioners in town."

I used to think she might be, er, bulls----ing us all. She isn't, though. She really DOES know her village geography. And she has a sharp memory regarding the history -- both good and bad -

- of families and incidents that have happened in Scotia since her birth in 1923. Fires, weddings, political events, church happenings and, yes, even scandals, are topics she can fill a person in on with ease. She has been a widow since November of 1961 when her beloved husband, former Scotian and United States Marine Charles Kelefant, died of a heart ailment. But Mom Kelefant's obvious zest for life and love of her family have kept her active to this day.

I am not one to let such a resource on Scotia go unused. I asked Mom Kelefant if she might sit down with me one afternoon and look over and comment on some hundred-or-so pictures from the past taken of village streets, buildings and people. It was kind of a make-believe "walk" around the village. She was only too happy to comply with my request.

The following is a record of some of the conversation we enjoyed that early spring morning when Mom Kelefant examined the pictures with me:

* * *

Mohawk School, showing the South Ten Broeck Street entranceway, as it looked in 1980 before it was closed. The site is now used for apartment and condominium housing. (Larry Hart collection.)

Mary Kelefant closely studied a list of the various men who have served as Superintendent of Schools for the Scotia-Glenville school system for over a hundred years. Her face broke into a grin when she saw the name of B.W. Conrad, who was the school superintendent from 1927 through 1949.

112

"Oh sure, Mr. Conrad," she said, remembering something from long ago. "My sister Katharine (Sturdy) wanted badly to teach in our Scotia schools, but she couldn't get a job here. So for the first five years of her teaching career she taught in Corning. One year she had three sessions of kindergarten with 30 kids in each session. That's 90 kids in one year."

Katharine, however, was about to head home.

"One afternoon, my sister and I were sitting in the backyard of the house at 203 Glen on a hot summer day. Around the corner of the house walks Mr. Conrad! He apologized for the intrusion, then told Katharine he had an opening for her as a first-grade teacher at the Old Lincoln School (on Huston Street) if she wanted to start that fall. Well, Katharine really wanted to teach kindergarten, but she accepted the position."

Katharine Sturdy eventually moved to a position as kindergarten teacher at Sacandaga Elementary School and was a fixture there for years. Miss Sturdy, who died in 1990, taught for 37 years -- 32 of them in Scotia. Many a Scotia native remembers her.

"Someone saw me on Glen Avenue recently and thought I was Katharine," Mary Kelefant said. "I had to explain that, no, she had passed."

Kelefant looked at a photograph showing the exterior of the Ten Broeck Street entrance to Mohawk School -- now the site of condominiums.

"They used to have a short, outdoor Christmas concert near that entranceway in December," she recalled. "They also had them up here (Albermarle Road) at New Lincoln School down the street. I always remember the time we went to one and we were walking back home when we got the joyous news that Bill and Dot Swartz -- our good neighbors across the street -- had just had a baby girl and named her Wendy! One of the boys ran over to give us the news."

Mary took extra time examining some pictures taken in the early 1950s around the neighborhood of Riverside Avenue -- two

Looking west on Riverside Avenue in April of 1987, this area was once the scene of a raging fire along the banks of the Mohawk River. (Larry Hart collection.)

blocks south of her old home at 203 Glen. She was fascinated, and the memories came swiftly.

"My gosh. This reminds me --- I'll never forget -- the awful fire down there one year," she said. "I remember that whole riverbank caught fire. Some oil had leaked and caught fire down by what at that time was called the 'Hook Farm' because of the way the river hooked around the bend. Peter Ulrich had the (vegetable) farm and his brother, Art Ulrich, had the greenhouses and florist shop on Engleman Avenue a block below Charles Street. The reason I remember that particular fire so well was because I hurried down there to see it on my roller skates. Well, didn't I trip over the water hose and fall! Oh, Mary, such goings on! The hose was attached to that fire hydrant you see in this picture right here."

Mary Kelefant was handed a picture of another, more familiar, scene: the Abraham Glen House, now the site of the Scotia Library.

She smiled.

"I remember when Nita Savage, a language teacher in the high school, for a long time used to have an apartment in the upstairs of that building. I never had her for a teacher, but she was a nice lady."

Then Kelefant was shown two separate pictures -- taken many years apart -- of the since-demolished Teddy Building on Mohawk Avenue at the foot of Sacandaga Road (Route 147), that area now is the site of the CVS building and its parking lot.

"Oh, my gosh; the old Teddy Building," Kelefant said, grinning widely in delight at a photo from the 1920s. "Karl Heiner's wife lived in an apartment upstairs there for many years with her mother before she married Karl. And there's Hudson's Store. It was a grocery store that sold, you know, canned goods and produce. And there's the Heenan's Market, and Schafer's Store. My friend Earl Letts used to work in there -- a long time ago."

The Maalwyck House, a building so distinct that it has a

The old Teddy Building was once a part of Mohawk Avenue's framework at the foot of Sacandaga Road. The top photo reveals life in 1920, while the bottom picture is the way things looked there in 1987. The building was demolished in the 1990s and is now a parking lot and also the site of the CVS building. (Larry Hart collection.)

familiar state marker outside the white picket fence of the property, elicited more smiles from Kelefant.

"I went in there one time to get warm after sliding down the hill on my sled in the wintertime," she recalled. "My mother knew Mrs. Hartman, who lived there at the time. It's a beautiful house."

Not too many Scotia residents seem to remember the old Schenectady Boat Club. But when Kelefant saw a photograph of the club building and the Mohawk River, she was quick to provide information on the subject.

"Sure. It was down off of Washington Avenue --down behind what is now the sewer works by the river," she said. "I remember people used to all go down to watch the boat races down there."

The next old photograph which particularly captured her attention was one from 1926 showing Mohawk Avenue at the corner of Ten Broeck Street looking East toward Schenectady.

"There's the firehouse, of course, and there's what used to be Mather's Drug Store, and then Seth Siskin took it over," she said. "And there's Spitzer's. And Mrs. Hardt had a gift shop down there across from the Baptist Church. I remember Mrs. Hardt; I think she used to sing in our (St. Andrew's Episcopal) choir. Down the street here on the right used to be Barcelow's Store. It was a father and mother that ran the store and they had a son named Homer. He was a big kid, and he had something wrong with his arm -- like a backward elbow or something that turned the wrong way. Doctors couldn't do anything about it back then."

A photo of the old Odd Fellows Hall on Mohawk Avenue brought more memories.

"I remember I had dancing lessons in there with my friend Alberta Letts," Kelefant said. Then her eyes brightened with happiness as she picked up another picture -- this time of a little girl wearing a hat standing outside a house on Ten Broeck Street.

"Oh, my gosh ... there's little Thelma Ryan Truax," she said with a wide smile. "She lived kind of kitty-corner from us. She

The Maalwyck House on Mohawk Avenue is one of Scotia's oldest and finest homes. (Larry Hart collecion.)

was a few years younger than me but we used to play together a lot."

Kelefant had much the same reaction to a picture taken in the fellowship room of the First Baptist Church. The photograph showed then-Governor Franklin D. Roosevelt with a number of church members, including a young girl seated to the future president's left.

"Goodness, there's Dorothy Millard!" she said. "Look at her there so young! I went to her wedding, you know."

Mary Kelefant explained that perhaps one of the reasons she still knows the outlay of Scotia so well today is due to the fact that most of her life she has gotten places by walking. It's a Sturdy family trait. Her own parents, Richard Oswald Sturdy and Mary (Howell) Sturdy, never drove an automobile a day in their whole lives.

"It wasn't that unusual, in those days, for people not to drive or own an automobile," Kelefant said. "Dad never drove, and he didn't mind. One reason he didn't drive was because he lost the sight in one of his eyes when he was seven. He was playing that he was pitching hay with table forks and sofa pillows, and he accidentally was poked in the eye. His mother and father took him to a doctor, and the doctor was at a dinner party and told them to bring him in the first thing next morning. It was too late."

The Sturdy family still went places, however.

"Oh, we used to take a bus or someone would pick us up and drive us if we needed to go somewhere. The rest of the time, we just walked," Kelefant said.

One of her most vivid memories of her father is how he used to walk home from Schenectady every Christmas Eve with the family Christmas tree.

"Dad worked at ALCO, and when he got done with work on Christmas Eve, he'd buy a Christmas tree somewhere on Erie Boulevard and walk all the way home with it across the Western Gateway Bridge," she said. "We kids never saw the tree until the

119

The Schenectady Boat Club off of Washington Avenue on the banks of the mean, muddy Mohawk was once a bustling site for Scotians seeking water fun. (Larry Hart collection.)

This 1926 photo of Mohawk Avenue, looking east near the junction of Ten Broeck Street, shows the trolley tracks down the middle of the avenue. Note the firehouse on the left and First Baptist Church further down the street. (Larry Hart collection.)

The old Odd Fellows Hall at 251 Mohawk Avenue, shown here in a 1925 picture, was a heavily used facility in its day. It was destroyed by a fire in 1947. (Larry Hart collection.)

next morning. Mom and Dad used to put up the tree and decorate it all on Christmas Eve after we'd all gone to bed."

On one of those walks home from work, her father lost a new hat.

"Dad always wore the same old hat for years," she said, then grinned at the memory she was about to relate. "Finally one day, my mother talked him into getting a new hat. Well, he only had it a few days and he was so proud of it. But wouldn't you know he was walking home across the bridge after work one day and a big wind came up and blew the hat right off his head and down into the Mohawk River. There went the hat!"

Thanks for the memories, Mom Kelefant! It was nice walking and talking with you.

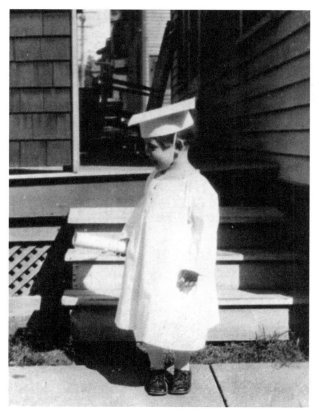

Thelma Ryan Truax, just 3 years old, is shown outside her South Ten Broeck Street home in 1923 after graduating from "Cradle Roll" in her nursery school. (Larry Hart collection.)

Then-New York State Governor Franklin D. Roosevelt is seated in the First Baptist Church's gymnasium on Sept. 9, 1929 after giving a dinner speech. Among those pictured with FDR, who would go on to become President of the United States, are young Dorothy Millard (left) and Elsie Kelley. (Larry Hart collection.)

124

Part VIII
Let Us Go Into the House of the Lord

Church steeples of many denominations have graced the skyline of the village of Scotia for all of us to see for many generations. Many of us who were raised in Scotia have had the opportunity to visit most or all of these houses of worship -- either for religious or secular reasons.

Me? I am an Episcopalian and am, in fact, at this writing studying the ministry. I am a postulant to the diaconate along with my wife, Mary Carol. However, whereas Mary Carol (Kelefant, Westad) Hart is a cradle Episcopalian, I am a hybrid Christian -- having been raised as a Baptist at the First Baptist Church of Scotia. Wait ... it gets more complicated: after 20 years as a Baptist, I converted to Roman Catholicism in 1967. Why, a lapse in faith? No, it's because I was about to be married to a Catholic girl and, since we anticipated having children, I didn't like the idea of having our household split into two religious halves. But then in 1991 when that 23-year marriage met a sad end, not long afterward I began dating Mary Carol and right away was drawn not only to her but to her Episcopalian church -- St. Andrew's.

There. That's enough of that, and if it sounds to you as though I was a mixed-up fellow following God around all those years, you're looking at it backwards -- it was quite the other way around. God, you see, was patiently following ME around.

Let's take a closer look at the history of each of the old churches located inside the village limits. Again, I refer to the 1914 "Scotia" booklet written by Nicoll and Cole and also to files kept by my late father for much of the factual information which follows:

ST. JOSEPH'S CHURCH

Roman Catholics in Scotia in the late 1800s either traveled to masses held in Schenectady or attended Catholic services held in Good Templars Hall. That all changed in the early 1900s when nine lots on First Street were purchased at a cost of $15,000, and a parish house and hall were erected.

The first service held in the new hall took place on Easter Sunday in 1909, with the Rev. T.H. Judge. The current, original red brick church building, which underwent extensive renovation and annexation in the 1990s, was built in 1926 following the completion of the hall and parish house.

That hall, torn down in the 1970s, was known as Placid Hall, and for many years was one of Scotia's most recognizable structures. Myself, I remember going to dances there as a teen, and also playing basketball on the wooden-floor gymnasium there. (I once played in a pickup game there one afternoon when all we had was one basketball -- mine -- and it was kind of bald from being used mostly outdoors on concrete and asphalt. At one point in the game, the ball bounded off to the left of the basket nearest the stage and landed on one of those old, metal water heaters along the wall. The ball popped a hole. We all heard this hiss-s-s-s-s noise, and that was the end of the game that day because nobody else had another basketball.)

St. Joseph's today is a beautiful church, and it is filled with zealous, earnest Christian people. I attended a musical service there a few years ago in which all the church choirs in Scotia were invited to take part -- and they did. It was a wonderful Sunday afternoon of soothing and inspiring religious music.

SCOTIA UNITED METHODIST CHURCH

This church originally was called the Scotia Methodist Episcopal Church, since it was affiliated with the Episcopal faith. The current building on North Ten Broeck and Catherine

A horse-drawn carriage pulls up in front of the St. Joseph's Church and rectory on First Street. Year unknown. (Larry Hart collection.)

Streets was dedicated on Nov. 29, 1903, with the Rev. E.P. Stevens celebrating at the service as Presiding Elder.

Although (as I stated earlier) I was a Baptist during my youth and teen years, I attended Sunday services at the Methodist church quite often -- especially when I was in high school -- because my good friend, Russ Hawkins, and his family were faithful members there. Also, I was a member of the Methodist church boys' basketball team which competed in the Church League at the Schenectady YMCA. My own Baptist church did not have a team at this point in time, so I chose to play for the Methodist team, which incidentally was coached by Russ' father, Ken Hawkins Sr. (who taught sixth grade at Sacandaga School right across the hall from my mother's room.) Therefore, I had to go to Sunday School classes there in order to play for the Methodists.

I enjoyed that brief Methodist church experience very much, and may I say not just because of the basketball involvement -- although of course that was part of it. I found the services and the family feeling of attending the church very similar to what I had long come to know at the Baptist church.

Sharon (Hartley) Dunlap has fond memories of the Scotia United Methodist Church ... even if one particular memory was a bit embarrassing!

"The first time I got married was at the Methodist church -- which I attended my whole childhood up until I was 24 years old," Dunlap said. "What happened was that the limousine wound up going down the wrong way on the one-way street on Center Street. The driver wasn't from around here, and I had just gotten married, so I wasn't paying attention to where he was going."

FIRST REFORMED CHURCH

This gorgeous church and grounds, perched high on Collins Street and overlooking Collins Lake and the entire park, is one of the first sights one sees when entering Scotia from the East.

It's trademark steeple is visible from points far away, such as windows on the higher floors of the west wings of Ellis Hospital.

The original Reformed church was constructed in 1822 and was dedicated on July 19 of that year

The original First Reformed Church of Scotia, with old Butler Hall and the cemetery, is shown in this 1940 photograph. The original church was destroyed in a 1943 fire. (Larry Hart collection.)

with Rev. Dr. A. Yates, the vice president of Union College, preaching the first sermon there. The church burned on Dec. 28, 1943, in one of the worst fires in Scotia's history, then was rebuilt ... with the first service (attended by 800 persons) held on Palm Sunday, 1952.

The church's annual Dutch Fair, held each year in mid-September, has long been a tradition to which Scotians flock in order to enjoy yard-sale bargains, food, games and simply meeting with friends old and new.

FIRST BAPTIST CHURCH

Ah. My old church on Mohawk Avenue. And what a place dear to my heart it is to this day. My mother, Ruth (Brooks) Hart, is one of the oldest living members of the church and a lifelong member. On April 18,

The new First Reformed Church of Scotia ... in a 1956 photograph. (Larry Hart collection.)

129

This early photograph from 1890 shows Mohawk Avenue looking northwest, with the steeple of the First Baptist Church visible in the middle of the photo. The shot was taken from the area known as "the campground" at the rear of the Glen Sanders Mansion. (Larry Hart collection.)

2004, the church held a special memorial service for my father, who like my mother had served the church for many years in a number of capacities, including choir member and church historian.

I grew up listening to the usually gentle but inspiring sermons of Rev. Raymond Rogers (now deceased) spoken from that pulpit, and I was baptized -- by immersion, the Baptist way, of course -- there in September of 1955 by Rev. Rogers. A bible (an old King James version) which I still use today was given to me by the church that very day.

The Baptist church is one of the oldest and most familiar buildings in the village. The church actually was organized on June 20, 1840, as the First Baptist Church of Glenville and was incorporated as the First Baptist Church of Scotia in 1885. The present church building was completed in 1872, replacing the original smaller, wooden structure.

There is so much I could say about this wonderful, old church. I had a very good time growing up there, feeling safe within its walls whether it was sitting with my parents, maternal grandparents and sister in the church service, being in Sunday School classes as a young boy or going to BYF (Baptist Youth Fellowship) meetings on Sunday evenings.

This, too, may seem an odd memory to add here, but add it I must: I have always enjoyed hearing the church bells pealing at dusk -- a kind of subtle reminder that God is always with us, if you will. One of my fondest memories of growing up in Scotia is this: I am a 9 or 10-year-old boy playing in a pickup baseball game with maybe Russ Hawkins, Bill Vazal, Albert Gates, Grant Downs, Dennis Madden and other boys on the old ball diamond at Mohawk School across the street from my house on a warm spring evening. The sun has already gone down, it's getting almost too dark to see, and suddenly off in the distance -- but loud and clear -- I hear the chimes at my Baptist church playing a couple of old hymns like "A Mighty Fortress is Our God," or "Holy, Holy, Holy."

The front and east side of the First Baptist Church on Mohawk Avenue, as it looked in 1918. (Larry Hart collection.)

Back in the winter of 1936-37, the First Baptist Church had a women's basketball team -- and a very good one! In front row, from left, are: Quinda Corino, Eileen Thompson, Sylvia Ratliffe, Elsie Ransom and Frances Emerson. Second row, from left, are: Ruth Hartman, Emma Murray, Loraine Bryce, Earl J. Winders (coach), Emily Emerson, Evelyn Ratliffe and Ruth Letts. Missing from photo is Evelyn Keller. (Larry Hart collection.)

This memory was brought back to me only last summer when, as a 56-year-old, I was playing in a men's recreation game at University at Albany on July 2nd. With the sun having long-since set and with darkness gathering, I was out in right field watching teammate Jim Dalton pitch to what would be the final batter of the day when suddenly the UAlbany campus carillon chimes began to announce that it was 9 p.m. The fond memory of being a young boy in my hometown so long ago listening to my church chimes pealing came flooding back to me. It was quite an emotional experience, and I had to fight back tears to watch the final out being made on an easy grounder to shortstop.

OUR REDEEMER LUTHERAN

This lovely little church on the corner of Reynolds Street and Glen Avenue is one of Scotia's newer churches. The church, according to information on its own website, began as a Sunday school class in Scotia Theater in 1924 as a mission of Zion Lutheran Church of Schenectady. The congregation was formed in 1925 with services in the basement of the present church, and the building was completed in 1934. An education building was added in 1959, and a second floor and sanctuary renovation project was finished in 1995.

ST. ANDREW'S EPISCOPAL CHURCH

My new home of St. Andrew's on Sacandaga Road and Third and Fourth Streets, which in a very real sense has become kind of my extended family, actually began as a mission church. Episcopalians in Scotia used to attend services held at the Odd Fellows Hall on Mohawk Avenue or the Red Men's Hall on Schonowee Avenue until the first service as an official mission church was held -- appropriately enough -- on St. Andrew's Day (Nov. 30) -- in 1909.

* * *

Rev. William Gray sat in a comfortable chair in the lounge of his beloved St. Andrew's Church one sunny Tuesday spring morning in 2004 following the bi-weekly men's breakfast and eucharist. The rotund, kind 78-year-old priest reflected on his 25 years as rector at the Scotia church by starting at the beginning.

Rev. William Gray

"I came here in April of 1962 ...," Gray said, then added with a smile that slowly broke across his face, "... and when Bishop Brown told me he had recommended that I come to St. Andrew's in Scotia, I had to get out a map to see where Scotia was, because I didn't know."

Actually, Gray's own hometown of Rensselaer -- a similar-sized community directly across from Albany on the other side of the Hudson River -- was only about 40 miles from Scotia. He attended -- and was ordained at -- Christ Church of the Epiphany in Rensselaer, the same church where his own mother and father were married.

"I had been priest-in-charge at two small parishes in the northern part of the state. Father Crosby here at St. Andrew's had been thinking of retiring, and the bishop nominated me as a possible successor to Father Crosby. He asked me to drive to Scotia and take a look at it. Charlie Betts, who was clerk of the vestry here, invited me to a meeting that night. Shortly afterward, I got a letter from the vestry informing me that they wanted me to succeed Father Crosby. I said 'Yes,' and I have never regretted my decision."

Gray stepped down in 1987 after a colorful and productive tenure as rector of St. Andrew's. He now serves as Pastor Emeritus at the church and is an active member, taking part in many church programs as well as serving as advisor to current rector Rev. Michael Neufeld and deacon, Rev. Richard Lehmann.

"Father Crosby was an easy man to follow here, because he had vision," Gray said, his expression turning more serious.

135

"What he did pastorally for his people was incredible. It made all the difference in the world to come in here and be able to build on what he had already prepared. Father Crosby saw to it in his tenure that there was a building fund established to begin the construction and additions that had to be done here. When I got here, there was already $10,000 in that fund."

During Gray's own successful stint at St. Andrew's, the church bought properties on Third and Fourth Streets and built additions to accomodate a growing parish family and to meet religious education needs. Gray also saw a greater need before him, one that applied not just to St. Andrew's but to all of Scotia.

"When I got here in 1962, an obvious need I saw was to secure a housing facility for the senior citizens. There were a large number of seniors in this congregation, and they had real worries about their future because housing was tight in Scotia, and there was no place for them to go once they were no longer able to take care of themselves."

In what may well be Gray's finest legacy to Scotia, he became the lightning rod of a long, two-decade struggle on the part of himself, St. Andrew's and community leaders to see the rise of the six-story senior housing project now known as Holyrood House on Huston Street and Fourth and Fifth Streets -- two blocks down from St. Andrew's.

"I had already been to the Division of Housing and Urban Development for New York State and was talking to them about our need in Scotia," Gray said. "But this anxiety had no real focus for awhile; it took some time to get organized and get things moving."

An original hope of Gray's was to acquire more property on the block and build a 10-story housing facility for seniors which would also include a parish house for the church. It didn't happen.

"People in the church said to me, 'Father Gray, are you nuts? Do you realize if we did that and built it there the mayor's house (then-Mayor John Ryan lived at the corner of Third Street) would never see the sun again?' So, very clearly, that original idea wasn't going to be feasible. To my regret, we didn't do it."

Instead, the church's and community's attention turned to the rundown Old Lincoln School and surrounding grounds -- the eventual site of the current Holyrood House.

"All of it couldn't have happened if our vestry hadn't followed the lead of what had transpired," Gray said. "The planning board decided to go in that direction. We had a long fight ahead of us, because we were denied zoning at first and had to sue to get zoning. It was finally approved by court."

The first proposal for the housing facility called for a 10-story structure, but it was a concern to the fire department for safety reasons. Architect George Vickey came up with a revised plan calling for six stories, which met with everyone's approval.

Gray, who served as chairman of the committee for Holyrood for 17 years before construction even began, ought to take a very deserving bow for all he did to get Holyrood (which means Holy Cross in Old English) built. But he will not, instead diverting the kudoes to others. Gray credits his parish with having the building become a reality after almost a score of years as a mere vision.

"It never would have happened if it weren't for this church vestry and the parish community," Gray said. "In all of those years I was chairman and I had to drive to HUD headquarters in New York City and Buffalo on a weekly basis, this vestry voted to pay for every phone call, every printing expense, and for my travel. And (now-deceased) Congressman Sam Stratton in D.C. deserves a lot of credit, too. He was one of the most active people pushing the office in Washington for this project, and we needed his help because everything we designed had to meet with the federal government's approval because they were going to fund the building."

When the building finally was completed, Gray was made Chief Executive Officer of the 96-apartment senior facility.

The completion of Holyrood House was hardly Gray's sole

Holyrood House, located at Huston Street and Fourth and Fifth Streets, finally became a reality after many years of dedicated work on the part of Rev. William Gray, currently Pastor Emeritus of his beloved St. Andrew's Episcopal Church of Scotia. This photo was taken in 1989. (Larry Hart collection.)

impact on St. Andrew's and the village as a whole, however. Gray's involvement with the community life and leadership of his parish was exemplary -- especially for a man who originally had no plans for a life as a priest.

"I was 16 when I graduated from high school in Rensselaer in 1942," Gray said. "At that time, I had no interest in studying the ministry. What did I want to do? I wanted to attend the U.S. Naval Academy in Annapolis, Md., but was turned down because I didn't meet the requirement of having 20-20 eyesight. I'm nearsighted, you see."

Disappointed, Gray instead enlisted in the Navy, serving in the Phillipines during World War II with the Seabees. He was a stevedore, loading and unloading Navy ships.

The whole course of his life changed irrevocably during his military hitch. Gray befriended a chaplain who was an Episcopal priest. That friend inspired him to consider an ordained life as a deacon once he returned home.

Gray took the friend's advice to heart, enrolling at Siena College on the G.I. Bill. After earning his Bachelor's degree in Liberal Arts, he pursued the Holy Orders and became first a deacon (on June 6, 1954), then a priest, of the Albany Episcopal Diocese.

"I felt God was calling me. That's why I did it. But to this day, I wonder if I did the right thing. I think it's just that God had his own plan for me. I wanted to be a Naval officer; he wanted me to be a priest. It hasn't been a bad experience. There has been a lot of joy, but also a lot of sorrow."

Gray has outlived both his beloved wife, Maribel, and their son, James. A daughter, Ruth, is all that remains of his nuclear family. Those sad deaths -- to people closest to him -- are not entirely what Gray was referring to, though, when he spoke of sorrow.

"By lots of sorrow, I mean situations when people get mad and move themselves out of the church, because I'm the priest and they don't like the way I do things. It has happened; and believe me, it hurts," Gray said. "But all I know is -- for the people I worked with here at St. Andrew's and responded to me -- the caring for other people is what God calls us all to do. He wants us to hold each other up; it's a feeling that, for me, is always there."

Sometimes his role as priest has been extremely difficult. Gray was asked if he thought it was especially hard to be a priest and spiritual leader of a flock during the early 1960s -- when President John F. Kennedy was assassinated, the Cold War with Russia was heating up, and the threat of nuclear war hung over everyone's head.

"Yes, it was a difficult time to be a priest then," Gray answered. "But I think even more difficult than that, for me, were the Vietnam War years that followed afterward. I had some families here with strong military backgrounds supporting the war effort, and I also had many whose children were opposed to the Vietnam War and were very vocal about it. My (son) Jim was one of those kids in the high school who was saying out loud that if he were ever drafted, he'd go to Canada. As a veteran myself, and as the father of a son, I had my own views on Vietnam which I kept to myself. But as rector here, I had to minister to all these people with very polarized views. A priest, you must understand, is often a person caught in the middle. That's the way it is for a priest. It hasn't changed one bit over the years."

Yes, but from the St. Andrew's community and from the village of Scotia, Father Gray -- Thank you! We're glad you found your way from Rensselaer to Scotia. We owe you a great debt.

Part IX
You Mean There Are Other Sports Besides Baseball?

In a previous chapter, I pretty much chronicled my lifetime passion for the sport of baseball. To me, all other recreational activities, noble as they may be, are simply games which pale by comparison.

I know ... it has everything to do with the way in which I was attracted to baseball in my youth, I suppose. My family was baseball-crazy, and I lived across the street from a school playground where kids played baseball all the time. Perhaps if I had been raised by a mom and dad who loved tennis, hockey or football, my outlook today might be different. I don't know.

Having said that, everyone knows that Scotia is certainly known for its success in a wide range of sports at the high school level. During the years in which I was in junior high and high school (and for a short time afterward), the varsity football teams coached by Dick McGuire enjoyed tremendous fan appeal and success. McGuire, a stern, no-nonsense former U.S. Navy man, would go on to become the high school prinicipal for a long tenure after many years as a physics teacher. He had a reputation, undeserved in my opinion, as a tough, mean-spirited man. But if you got to know him, one could see that the grouchy exterior was a facade covering a very sincere, gentle heart. I have always liked Dick McGuire, although I must admit I didn't really get to know him until after I was out of high school and became a sports writer. He and I did not always agree on things when I was a reporter, and we tangled once in a while over issues like how Section II money was spent and not spent, but I always respected his point of view.

McGuire's teams, it seemed, either won the old Western Conference (league before the Suburban Council and Foothills

Council) title every year or were right in the thick of the race right up to the end. The home games at the new high school were all on Saturday afternoons in those days, of course, before the lights and new all-weather track were installed in 1990.

Before the new field behind the school was laid out, however, I remember going to home football games on the old field at Collins Park in the 1950s. It was a blast! The field was laid out east to west in the bowl behind the library, and if you were a kid like I was, it was pretty easy to sneak in and watch the game without paying. The entrance was sectioned off with ropes, but if you waited

Dick McGuire, fiery football coach (as well as a physics teacher and in later years principal) of Scotia High, walks off the field at Niskayuna with linemen Bruce Senn, left, and Dick Olin after the final game of the 1963 season. (1964 Scotia High yearbook photo.)

for an opportune moment once the game had begun, you could duck under the ropes when the man tending the entrance was watching the action on the field. Then you could use that money your mother gave you for your ticket on an extra hot dog or two!

Basketball was always a prime attraction in town, too. (Boys basketball was IT, however, because in the 1950s and 1960s girls had only intramural sports for a recreational outlet. Sadly, when girls' varsity sports were in their infancy all over the country in the early 1970s, they faced a long growing process -- not just in Scotia, but everywhere -- to reach a status of equality and acceptance with boys' sports. One could argue that in 2004 that process is still ongoing.

Scotia's boys' basketball teams were always competitive in the years I was in junior high and high school. But in 1963-64, the year I was a senior, coach Dick Causey's guys did the unthinkable: they won not only the Western Conference title but the Class A crown of the section. It was preposterous, really. Scotia, one of the smallest Class A schools, won the whole bag of marbles that year -- not Linton, not Troy, not someone else. Scotia won.

The village was crazy that whole late-February, early-March week that Scotia was knocking on the door. The late-round games were played at neutral Mechanicville in a large (for its time), two-tiered gymnasium in a building which over the years has served as a middle school and elementary school. It seemed everyone in Scotia went to the semifinals and the final. Scotia, led by center Butch Hurley, sharpshooting guard Eddie Luberda and energetic point guard Corky Bleser, got the job done by upsetting Linton in the semis before finishing off Bethlehem in the championship game.

I can still see the wild, post-game celebration of players and fans on the court as if it were yesterday instead of 40 years ago. Then when the team left the floor, we proud fans waited for the team to get showered and dressed so we could congratulate them again when they left the locker room to come to the bus.

If you were a kid or teen in those days, too, there were plenty of places to play recreation basketball in town -- both pickup games and in fun, but competitive, leagues. There was a rec league in the Eighth Grade Building (now Schenectady Christian School) run by junior high phys ed instructor Dick Rollins on certain winter weeknights. And many churches in town had teams in the Church League at the Schenectady YMCA.

Scotia's varsity basketball team did the unthinkable in the winter of 1963-64, winning the Section II Class A championship. Front row, from left, are: Sam Strauss, Corky Bleser, Ron Acton, Eddie Luberda, Wayne Fetter and Tom Onderchain. Back row, from left, are: coach Dick Causey, manager Jim Mahoney, John Carpenter, Ralph Stevens, Butch Hurley, Andy Techy, Larry Thomas and manager Tom Castner. (1964 Scotia High yearbook photo.)

Myself, I never cared too much for basketball until 10th grade when I got into it because of my deep friendship with Russ Hawkins, whose father (Ken Sr.) was coach of the Methodist team. So for the last three years in school, I played for that Methodist team with Hawkins, Albert Gates, Jack Rodber, Bob Ostrander, Dick Hoffman and other guys. I didn't have much talent or success with basketball, but I sure had fun! And the competition ranged from poor to excellent. We used to beat some small church teams pretty easily, but in turn we also were given many a come-uppance by good teams like Scotia Reformed. My goodness, that Reformed team, coached by a man named Gil Kelly, beat us a few times by scores like 100-29! I'm not kidding. They had kids like Arkley Mastro, Mark Lansing, Pete Obman and Greg Perry, and they'd run around us, over us and through us!

Bowling, like baseball a sport to which I was introduced at an early age by my parents and materal grandparents, was another activity for Scotia kids of the 1950s and 1960s to enjoy. Scotia Lanes (now Rolling Greens) on Mohawk Avenue was a lively place where a kid or teen could go and safely hang out, either to bowl or to watch older bowlers compete in fast leagues.

As far as being a participant, for Alan Hart the teen-ager in the 1960s it was strictly baseball, more baseball, bowling and rec basketball. That is, until one fateful September morning in 1963 when I was sitting in homeroom in our all-boys homeroom in the A wing of the high school with our teacher, Mr. Larry Rainey. Suddenly, the announcements were being read over the intercom. Others kids were talking and I really couldn't hear one particular announcement very clearly, but I thought it said something about tryouts for the first Scotia High soccer team being held that day after school, and if you were interested to either just show up or to see coach Karl Gerstenberger.

I turned around and asked Jim Henderson, seated in back of me, if I had heard correctly. He said yes, and immediately my mind created some pictures of me running up and down a field, kicking a ball and scoring a goal. I was definitely interested, because I had already met coach Gerstenberger. He was my German teacher and a very, very nice man. Once I found out some of my best friends -- Arkley Mastro, Albert Gates, Tom Reep and Don Timm -- were going out for it, too, I was even more excited!

It was a great time. We didn't have uniforms (until late in the season), so we wore gym clothes. We didn't know whether or not we were going to be recognized as a varsity team and thus get varsity "letters" we could sew on our jackets or sweaters (we did!) Most of all, none of us kids knew a damned thing about soccer or how to play it. None, that is, except a foreign exchange student from Argentina named Ricardo Capparelli. He was a good kid, he could run and he had a rocket of a shot. We also had in Karl Gerstenberger a coach who knew and loved the game, and he was eager to teach it to a bunch of kids who would listen.

For most of us, soccer was something European and strange. The ball was yellow and made of uncoated leather, and it would get very heavy when it got wet, which it often did. Unlike today's plastic-coated light balls, the ones we used weighed a ton and would hurt your foot when you kicked one. (That's partly because we didn't realize, at first, that you were supposed to kick with your instep, not your big toe.)

What fun we had! I remember Mr. Gerstenberger's immense patience with us as we struggled to learn this sophisticated game. He'd get frustrated with us in those early workouts when we'd all swarm to the ball wherever it was on the field, and he'd scream "Stay in your positions, boys ... stay in your positions!"

And he had us run, run and run. We all got into tremendous shape. After awhile, we didn't mind all the running. It didn't seem too bad, after all. We'd be out for practice in the rain, wind and cold while the football team was inside watching film or something, and we'd taunt the football players for being "spastics" or "pansies." They would give it right back, of course. This rivalry with the football team was mostly in good fun, you

Scotia's very first varsity soccer team is shown in the fall of 1963. Identifiable persons in the photo are as follows: First row, from left: Alan Hart, Dick Brearton, Jim Engel, Gary Giebel, Arkley Mastro, coach Karl Gerstenberger, Ricardo Capparelli, ?, ?, Jim Pritchard and Greg Way. Second row, from left: Jim Light, Dave Whitman, Bill Hoppmann, Dean Sharbaugh, Tom Godbout, John Huston, Tom Reep, Don Timm and Don Lawyer. Identifiable in third row are: Gary Curcio (fourth from left), Albert Gates (second from right) and George Vollmer (extreme right.) (1964 Scotia High yearbook photo.)

understand, but there was also a real base of resentment, too, from myself and many other soccer players who didn't like being treated as second-class citizens in school compared with the football players who were fussed over with pep rallies, assemblies ... all that kind of hooraw. I'll be very honest: I actually used to root for the opposing school to beat Scotia's football team, unless I happened to be covering the game for the Gazette (I was a correspondent for the paper in those days) and had to be neutral.

But we had fun with that inaugural soccer season. There was a definite feeling of pride that you were part of something important and historic -- the first-ever team of a new sport at Scotia High.

It was a good team, too. With Capparelli our only real offensive threat, we had trouble scoring goals. But we had a good defense, and the mainstay of that defense was Mastro -- a fearless kid who played "sweeper" right in front of the goalkeeper. Nobody on the team appreciated Mastro's talent more than I did, because I was the starting goalie. I only had to stop whatever got past Arkley, and not much got past him!

We played five games that fall, and we won two of them. A 2-3 record might not sound that impressive, but it was. We had started something on which future teams could build. Nine years later, when Scotia won the sectional Class B title, I was proud, as I'm sure other soccer alumni from that 1963 team were proud.

I can never thank Karl Gerstenberger enough for having had the foresight and patience that fall to teach a team of bumbling kids a new sport. It was a time in my life which I'll always remember with great fondness, and I'm sure I'm not alone in that one.

* * *

It's been over 40 years now since the night in early March of 1964 when Corky Bleser rejoiced on the gym floor in Mechanicville when he helped Scotia High beat Bethlehem to win the Section II Class A basketball tournament championship.

Yes, it's been over 40 years. But Bleser, the team's savvy and talented point guard, remembers as if it were yesterday.

Fred "Corky" Bleser

"Everybody in town and in the newspapers -- they were surprised at what we did. We weren't. We knew we had a good eam, and we knew we were going to do it," Bleser said during a May afternoon chat at the Glenville Queen diner. "The hard part, I guess, was beating Linton in the semifinals. But I knew all those Linton guys very well from playing at the YMCA and in Central Park, because I used to go over to Schenectady a lot, visiting my aunt. We weren't in awe of those Linton guys."

Bleser recalled the cool confidence, too, which emanated from Scotia's fine coach -- Dick Causey, who died a few years ago.

"Dick Causey was a nice guy, and a great guy to play for," Bleser said, sadness suddenly evident in his expression. "He was fair with us all, as far as who would play and who wouldn't. Age and experience didn't count for everything. I was lucky as a junior to start with guys like Butch Hurley and Eddie Luberda. I was a junior, and there were a few guys who were seniors who weren't too happy that I was in the starting lineup instead of them, but I just decided it was their problem and not to let it bother me. I just enjoyed playing for Dick Causey, because he gave me an opportunity."

Bleser credits still another coach, Joe Ketchum, with having a major impact on his basketball career.

"Dick Causey kind of fine-tuned the way I played point guard, but it was Mr. Ketchum -- my ninth-grade coach -- who really changed the way I played. He got me going with my left hand. He convinced me that I was too prone to use my right hand and to go to my right all the time. He told me if I was going to get better, I had to start using my left hand, and thanks to him, I did."

It all culminated in 1964 with a Western Conference championship and, finally, the unthinkable: the Section II Class A title. (Note: in 1964, there was no such thing as a state tournament, as is the case today.)

"It was quite a thrill, of course," Bleser said of the drive to the top in 1963-64. "It was great how we wound up playing Bethlehem (in the final), because we weren't supposed to beat Linton and Bethlehem wasn't supposed to beat Troy. Linton had Rusty Vitallo, Paul Heiner, John Modest, Phil Tama ... and as I said, I knew all those guys. So beating them made it all that much sweeter."

Bleser took extra delight in beating Linton, too, because of a perceived slight from the late and great Linton coach, Walt Przybylo.

"Przybylo said something to his team a few days before the game -- and it got back to me --about how I supposedly always go to my right. So of course the whole left side was wide-open all

Corky Bleser (35, at right) watches as teammate Larry Thomas (15) snares a rebound during a game against Draper sometime in the 1963-64 season. Other Scotia players are Andy Techy, left, and Butch Hurley (31.) (1964 Scotia High yearbook photo.)

night, and I just had one of the best games I ever had. I remember Butch got into early foul trouble that game, which we hadn't counted on. But another senior -- John Carpenter -- came off the bench and he did a great job. He was something like 6-foot-5, and we had Andy Techy who was 6-5 and Larry Thomas, another big bull, crashing the boards. Even Eddie Luberda was 5-10 or 5-11, so I could get away with being 5-8. I think being short actually helped me that whole season, because being a smaller player, the other teams would naturally look at 6-6 Butch Hurley and say, 'we have to stop him,' and that would leave people like me open."

Bleser remembers being almost "assured" four assists per ballgame, thanks to a set play designed in the preseason by Causey.

"In those days, you tossed the ball up for a center jump to start each quarter," he said. "Well, Butch would tip the ball to Eddie, who was positioned near the top of the key, and I'd go into a corner. So when Eddie caught the tip, he'd pass it over to me and I'd pass it to Butch cutting to the basket, and he'd either get a dunk or a layup, and I'd get an assist. Usually four a game, actually."

The oddity of that super season on 1963-64 was that, after that glorious Class A title win, the Tartans were beaten by Ballston Spa -- the Class B champion, in the old Class A-B playoff. In those pre-state tournament days, the A-B (and C-D) playoffs were rather meaningless games simply meant to give each champion one more game to play.

Scotia had already beaten Ballston Spa, a Western Conference foe, twice during the regular season. Those same village fans and sports writers who had been so surprised to see Scotia win the A title were just as shocked to watch the Tartans lose the A-B game.

"Hey, it happens," Bleser said with an annoyed shrug. "People forget it's a tough game, and Ballston Spa was a good team that we had to play well against to beat twice already that season. Whenever you have to beat somebody three times, it's always tough. That's been proven over and over again many times."

As was the case with baseball, playing alongside older players at an early age, Bleser credits older boys in his Reynolds Street/Mohawk School neighborhood with having helped him learn the game of basketball.

"I grew up in a kind of basketball-crazy neighborhood. There was an outdoor court at old Mohawk School. It wasn't quite big enough for a regular 5-on-5 fullcourt game. But there was always a game going on down there, and I was usually part of it."

Bleser not only played, but learned from the older boys. He learned quickly. He soon became a fixture on the Mohawk court.

"We used to play until it got dark and couldn't see anymore," he said. "I used to have neighbors who used to sit on their front porches on summer nights. When they heard me coming down the street bouncing my basketball to come home, they knew it was time to go inside."

Bleser remembered one night when he had to go home early. Two nights, actually.

"One night I was playing with the older kids, and Bruce Oudt -- a really big kid -- was under the basket. I cut past him on the baseline and all of a sudden ran into one of those big metal poles that held up the baskets, and I got pretty dazed. The game stopped and I said to Bruce, 'Bruce, you better walk me home. I'm seeing double, and I feel kind of dizzy.' "

Bleser saw a doctor that evening, and the physician advised him to avoid sports and running for three days.

But the next day, of course, the irrepressible Bleser predictably was back out on the Mohawk School outdoor court. For awhile, anyway!

"My mother was coming home in the car from work and saw me playing out there, he said smiling. "She stopped the car in the middle of the street, rolled down the window and yelled, 'Corky, you get in this car -- right now!' "

He went.

After his playing days at Scotia High ended, Bleser played basketball on base and squadron teams while serving in the U.S. Air Force. He had played recreation basketball as an adult, but not in recent years.

"Butch and Eddie and I used to play in a Rotterdam league," he said. "I enjoyed it, but it got to be too much with work constraints. And I wanted to be able to see as many of my son's games as I could."

Bleser's son, Mark, played varsity soccer and basketball at Burnt Hills High. Mark just completed his sophomore year at Johnson & Wales, R.I., where he is captain of the men's soccer team.

"My father used to be at all of my games when I was playing sports," Corky Bleser said. "I wanted to do the same for Mark. You know, he got a cracked bone in his neck as a freshman, but he came back and made all-conference and was tournament MVP, and now he's a captain. He's a tough kid."

A chip off the old block, in fact!

* * *

Arkley Mastro Jr. opened the cellophane bag of oyster crackers, poured the contents into the Manhattan chowder in the bowl in front of him as he sat in a Latham restaurant. He pondered the question which had just been put to him. The question had been "How is it that you didn't play on that 1963-64 Scotia High championship basketball team? After all, you did go on to stardom as a collegiate player at Clarkson. So ... why didn't you play that year in high school?"

Mastro picked up his soup spoon, swirled the spoon around in the bowl in order to get the crackers mixed in with the chowder, then replied, "Actually, there are two explanations why that happened."

Mastro, currently Glenville's Town Attorney and since 1987 a member of the Latham-based Gordon, Siegel Law Firm, explained.

"I was very interested in pool at that time. It was one of my favorite things to do," Mastro said. "I'll give you an example. One time, there was a high school field trip to the American Museum of Natural History in New York City. My buddy, the late Dave Kaestle, and I kind of hung back when the bus was unloading, and we managed to sneak away and instead went into the city to Ames' Billiard Parlor -- a place that was legendary for pool and billiards. We spent the afternoon there and snuck back in time to get back on the bus!"

Mastro got away with that particular pool-related hijink. On one other occasion, however, he was not as fortunate.

"I was on the JV basketball team as a junior, and (teammate) John Carpenter -- who also loved pool -- and I went to play a few games before practice. Well, we lost track of the time and we were late for practice. We had a tough coach -- Dick Herodes, and naturally he was ticked off when John and I rushed in to practice about 45 minutes late that day. He asked us why we were late, and John just looked him straight in the eye and said 'Arkley was in the middle of a run at the pool parlor and we couldn't leave.' Hey ... at least he was honest! Mr. Herodes wasn't amused; he had us run laps the whole rest of the practice."

A passion for pool was not the only blockade to a spot on that varsity basketball roster for Mastro.

"The other reason I didn't play was just that a few of us decided instead of going out for varsity we were just going to put our own team together and play in recreation leagues and have some fun. I liked Dick Causey well enough, but some of the guys didn't really like him. In other words, we were going to show him how good we were and what he was missing," Mastro said.

Then nodding as he managed an embarrassed smile, Mastro added, "So what happens? Dick Causey goes out and coaches the team to its best season in history. Yeah, I guess we really showed him!"

Mastro admits now he wishes he had played that season.

"It would have been nice," he said. "Truthfully, my (basketball) game matured toward the end of high school. I remember that senior year I was driving around the village with a friend, Chuck DiLella, one day and we stopped to talk to Andy Techy, who was shooting baskets in his own driveway. Andy had just made first-team, All-County, in the newspapers for his part in helping Scotia to the championship. I can't remember who challenged whom, but I got out of the car and played Andy one-on-one and beat him. Then we played a second game, and I beat him again. Then we played a third game, and I beat him worse. Chuck never let Andy forget that!"

(Sad note: Techy, who came to this country with his family in 1956 as a Hungarian refugee, died a few years ago.)

While Mastro did boycott varsity basketball, Mastro did compete in two varsity sports -- baseball and soccer -- at Scotia. If there are regrets now about having missed out on that memorable varsity basketball year of 1963-64, there are enough memories of his soccer experience to soften those regrets.

"I loved playing on that first soccer team. Karl Gerstenberger was a great guy and a lot of fun to play for," Mastro said. "I sure would like to have had the chance to play for him for four years, and I know it would have helped me in basketball, because soccer is a great companion sport for basketball. You do a lot of running in both sports."

Mastro covered a wide area of turf as "sweeper" on defense. He guarded that turf with a vengeance, and he got away long, accurate kicks to keep the ball away from the Scotia goal.

"I thought we had a great team. We gave a lot of experienced teams like Burnt Hills and Guilderland -- who expected to have an easy game with us -- a real run for their money. We seemed to get better with every game, too."

Part X
The Buhrmasters

On March 25, 1845, a child named Christian Heinrich Burmeister was born in Hille, a small farm village in central Germany. In 1871, Burmeister married Caroline Marie Louisa Krueger -- a young lady of the same village.

Soon afterward, the couple emigrated to the United States -- originally to the site of what is now Auriesville Shrine. The Burmeister couple had since changed its last name to "Buhrmaster," because that's the way the name was spelled on Christian Heinrich's discharge papers from the Prussian Army.

In Auriesville, on March 27, 1876, the couple's third child -- Johann Heinrich -- was born. Young Johann, who would later change his name to the Americanized John Henry Buhrmester (and, finally, Buhrmaster), moved to Saratoga County in 1885 upon the death of his mother. Eventually, John Henry Buhrmaster found his way to the quiet little village of Scotia where he began raising his family of three sons along with his wife, the former Cora Mae Ward of Glenville.

It is indeed Scotia's good fortune that this son of proud German immigrants chose to settle in Scotia, New York, because without a doubt the village's long and colorful history would not have been nearly the same. The community owes a great deal to the Buhrmaster family, which four generations later now is still giving back much to the village in the form of leadership, dignity and service.

Young J.H. Buhrmaster was educated in Saratoga public schools but left after eighth grade to become a farmer until 1900. Then he began a retail milk business and a grocery business from 1900 to 1912 when he became owner and operator of a retail coal, feed and building supply business in Scotia.

156

The Buhrmaster family of Scotia traces its roots to European soil. Christian Heinrich Burmeister and Caroline (Krueger) Burmeister both were born in the 1840s in the central German farm community of Hille, Germany. (Photo courtesy of the Buhrmaster family.)

The business evolved into the booming J.H. Buhrmaster Co., Inc., which is still in existence and a vital part of the area's economic picture.

J.H. Buhrmaster, who died in 1952, began a legacy of trust and service to the village of Scotia that he handed down to his youngest and only surviving son, Kenneth Buhrmaster, who passed the baton on even further to grandchildren and great-grandchildren who are active in Scotia business and community projects today.

Despite the success and prosperity of the Buhrmaster clan over the last century, family members have always responded generously to the needs and concerns of the rest of the people in the village.

It all began with John Henry Buhrmaster. Tony Dorazio Sr., whose own family tree is rooted deep into Scotia soil, speaks fondly of the mutual love and respect between his own family and the Buhrmasters.

Johann Heinrich Buhrmaster (who changed his name to John Henry) built a successful fuel and oil company -- still in operation today as the J.H. Buhrmaster Company, Inc. -- out of what began as a retail milk and grocery business in the early 1900s. (Photo courtesy of the Buhrmaster family.)

Dorazio, longtime original owner of Wayside Hardware and Garden Center on Sacandaga Road, normally has a very wide smile on his face during general conversation. However, change the topic of the conversation to the Buhrmaster family, and his countenance takes on a loving, reverent and thankful expression.

"Let me tell you something about the Buhrmasters," Dorazio said one spring afternoon. "During the Depresssion, my father -- his name was Alexander, but people called him 'Alec' -- was having a hard time just like everyone else. My father went to J.H. Buhrmaster -- Ken's father -- and told him that winter was coming on and he needed coal, but he couldn't pay him right away. He explained he worked for the New York Central railroad and only got paid every two weeks -- when he was working, that is. Well, J.H. told my father he'd see what he could do. You know, the NEXT morning my father looked out the window and there, next to the house, the coal was there! Our two families have had that mutual friendship and respect for each other for generations now."

Dorazio's story is a familiar one all over Scotia. J.H. Buhrmaster later became involved and instrumental in the growth of the First National Bank of Scotia, a landmark of Mohawk Avenue. He was one of the bank's founding directors, then served as vice- president from 1923 to 1936 and then as president beginning in 1936. Many Scotians had stories to tell their descendants about how the Buhrmasters helped them get through the demanding years of The Great Depression in the early 1930s.

Detroit, Mich., has its Ford family history. Hyannis Port, Mass., has its Kennedys.

Scotia has its Buhrmasters.

J.H. Buhrmaster, in addition to his accomplishments in the field of energy and heating and in banking, was a member of the New York State Assembly in 1932 and 1933. Buhrmaster also served three terms as supervisor for the Town of Glenville and served on the Schenectady County board of supervisors.

Kenneth Buhrmaster, J.H.'s youngest son, was born on June 15, 1915. (J.H.'s two eldest sons, Neil and Louis, died of tuberculosis as very young men.)

Kenneth Buhrmaster almost naturally assumed his father's role of successful businessman and community leader, serving

The huge white coal pockets on the J.H. Buhrmaster Company, Inc., grounds on Sacandaga Road, with the illuminated red letters at the top, were a familiar sight for miles during the mid-20th century. The coal pockets were torn down for safety reasons in 1987. (Photo courtesy of the Buhrmaster family.)

the community in many ways, including through church (Scotia United Methodist), service clubs (Scotia Rotary) and education (as two-time president of the Scotia-Glenville School Board, from 1950 to 1953, and again from 1956 to 1961.)

Kenneth and his wife of 66 years, the former Flower Sheldon, have three children -- sons Louis Henry Buhrmaster (64), James Roy Buhrmaster (59) and Lois Ann Seyse (55.)

Louis, since the retirement of Fred Lindsey in 1969, has served as president of the First National Bank. Jim, president of the J.H. Buhrmaster Company, Inc., in 2003 was elected to the Schenectady County Legislature.

It is a family whose members are all justifiably proud of the family's countless contributions to Scotia's history, but none of the members are quick to broadcast that pride. Actually, they don't have to be vocal about it; the many accomplishments speak for themselves.

Here is a just a partial list of the deeds of just some of the Buhrmaster family members concerning Scotia's history since John Henry Buhrmaster settled in Scotia about 100 years ago:

John Henry Buhrmaster (1876-1952) -- Charter member of Scotia Rotary when it was formed in 1929; active member of the Scotia United Methodist Church from early 1900s to his death in 1952, instrumental in building of the church's chapel in 1920, and a stained-glass window bearing the family's name is in the entranceway; was a nearly life-long mason; graduated from the General Electric Shop Apprentice System for Boys (sometime between 1901 and 1917);

Arthur Edward Buhrmaster (1888-1950) -- Son of Christian Heinrich Buhrmaster, who remarried (Marie Brandhorst, in 1888) after his first wife, Caroline Krueger, passed away in 1885; served on the original board of directors of the First National Bank; played a prominent role in the village in the 1920s and 1930s as officer for the J.H. Buhrmaster Company, campaigned for the New York State Senate in 1938 but was unsuccessful.

160

The Buhrmaster family has long been involved with Scotia Rotary, as the presence of both J.H. Buhrmaster (first row, second from left) and Kenneth Buhrmaster (top row, extreme left) in this photo of the 1939-40 club will attest. First row, from left: William Wayand, J.H. Buhrmaster, Louis Kinum, Dr. Ross Clark, Dr. Leo Snell, William Nicoll, Dr. Leslie Sullivan, Harley James, Ray Ballert, Harry Leisring, Dr. William Treder, Walter Rankin, Wilfred Stone, Charlie Pedrick. Second row, from left: Dr. Adolpson, Burt Quennell, Joseph Martinec Sr., Vernon Buys, Henry Nelson, James Nicoll, James Barstow, Dr. Elbridge Richardson, Hollis Witbeck, John Sigle, Rev. Morton Weller, ?, George Timm, George Eaton, Dr. Shannon, Fred Olin, Dr. Herman Galster, Paul Van Auken, Adson Haight. Third row, from left: Rev. Wright, Allyn Joslyn, Al Swanker, Dudley Rowledge, John Randall, Dusty Rhodes, Joseph Martinec Jr., William Moore, Dr. Nelson Rust, R.J. Pulling, Ernie Lehman, Mr. Fanstock, Dudley Hill, Angelo Alessandrini, Ken Parkis, James Gould, William Millard. Top row, from left: Kenneth Buhrmaster, Elwyn Roberts, Red Bishop, Lew Cornell, Dr. Perillo, Robert Zollner, Donald Hitchcock, T.K. Hymers, William Cassidy, William Churchill, Raymond Lunn, William Gilgore, C. Wilson Gillespie, Harold Hathaway, Harold Roberts, Dr. Von Borstell, Walter Gifford, Riley Coons. (Photo courtesy of the Buhrmaster family.)

Kenneth Buhrmaster (1915-present) -- Joined Scotia Rotary in 1937 at age 22, and is still a member. Served as president of the club in 1955-56; active in Scotia United Methodist Church for many years; has received incredible amount of community awards in his lifetime; in 1995 was honored by Syracuse University, his Alma Mater, with the Letterman of Distinction award. (other prominent Americans who have won this award include Jim Boeheim, Aaron Sorkin, Bob Costas, Dick Clark and William Safire.); joined the J.H. Buhrmaster Company right out of college in 1937 and was responsible for purchasing the company's first oil delivery truck; original board member of the Schenectady Economic Development Corporation; longtime volunteer fireman with the Scotia Fire Department; elected to the Scotia-Glenville School Board in 1948, served as president in 1950-53 and again in 1956-61; served as Chairman of the New York State Educational Conference Board from 1963 to 1969; Chairman of the New York State Bankers Association Retirement System in 1971-72, and has been a trustee and member of the Investment Committee of the association to this date; a member of the New York State Regents Appointed Committee of Education Leadership, in 1966 was appointed by Gov. Nelson E. Rockefeller to represent on the Education Commission of the States; received the State University of New York at Albany Distinguished Service Award in 1968; currently at age 88 is Chairman of the Board of the J.,H. Buhrmaster Co., Inc, and Chairman of the Board of Directors of the First National Bank of Scotia; has served as director, vice-president and trustee of the Schenectady Branch of the Capital District YMCA; was presented the Alexander Glen Award by the Village of Scotia in 1987 in recognition for long and faithful service to the people of Scotia; was honored with "Kenneth E. Buhrmaster Week" in Scotia in October of 1971 in recognition of his contributions to the community and his love for the village and its people; donates a scholarship award in his name to a member of each graduating class at Scotia High.

Sacandaga School second-grade student John Buhrmaster, right, and Flower Buhrmaster are on hand as Kenneth Buhrmaster is treated to cupcakes by third-grader Anne Brown during the village's observance of "Kenneth L. Buhrmaster week" during October of 1971. (Photo courtesy of the Buhrmaster family.)

Flower (Sheldon) Buhrmaster (1916-present) -- Wife of Kenneth, was a founding member of the Eucalyptus Garden Club of Scotia in 1958. (She is still active in the club today with her daughter, Lois Syse, and daughter-in-law, Judy Buhrmaster, and granddaughter-in-law Leslie (Jones) Buhrmaster; today, at age 88, continues to work in accounting for J.H. Buhrmaster Co., Inc.

Louis Buhrmaster (1939-present) -- Joined Scotia Rotary in 1964, was president in 1986-87; served as manager for the U.S. Rowing team for the 1959 Pan American Games in Chicago; president of the First National Bank of Scotia since 1969 (after beginning his career there as a parking lot attendant in 1956); former treasurer of J.H. Buhrmaster Company, Inc.; former member of the Metroplex board; past scoutmaster for Troop 62 in Scotia; past board member for Parkside YMCA; longtime District 4 Fire Commissioner; current vice-chairman of the Scotia-Glenville Economic Development Committee; vice-president of the Schenectady Industrial Corporation, treasurer for the Schenectady-Glenville Development Zone Administration Board, and director of the Scotia Relief Association; involved in the establishment of the Scotia Business Improvement District in 2000.

James R. Buhrmaster (1945-present) -- Member of Scotia Rotary since 1969, was president in 1978-79; led efforts to raise funds for the Scotia High sports program in the late 1980s after the budget was defeated and funding for sports programs were eliminated; current President of J.H. Buhrmaster Co., Inc.; former treasurer of First National Bank; active in American Field Service foreign exchange program (was himself an exchange student who spent a semester in Sweden in 1962 as a high school junior); was elected to the Schenectady County Legislature in November of 2003.

Lois (Buhrmaster) Seyse (1948-present) -- Currently Corporate Secretary at J. H. Buhrmaster Company, Inc., a position she has held for many years since returning from living in Alaska during the late 1960s; active in Girl Scouts in Scotia for many years.

Margaret "Mugsie" (Burch) Buhrmaster (1939-present) -- Former wife of Louis Buhrmaster, Margaret served as a Schenectady County Legislator for 18 years; first woman elected as chairman of legislature, receiving many local and national awards during her tenure.

John H. Buhrmaster (1964-present; great-grandson of John Henry, grandson of Kenneth and Flower, son of Louis and Margaret) -- Became Rotary member in 2000; became fourth-generation member of Buhrmaster family to work at First National Bank when he started as a teller there in 1986 right out of Syracuse University; also worked for the J.H. Buhrmaster Company, Inc., before that cleaning buildings and shoveling coal; New York State High School Track Official since 1985, currently treasurer of the association; current board member of Schenectady Employment Training Development Corporation, Capital Region Revolving Economic Developmnent Fund, New York Bankers East Title Company, Scotia Insurance Agency and Intercept Advisory Board.

Will Seyse (1950-present) -- Husband of Lois Buhrmaster, he is a former Mayor of Scotia and currently a trustee for the village.

Kenneth C. Buhrmaster (1969-present) -- Son of James and Sandra (Coons) Buhrmaster, grandson of Kenneth L. and Flower Buhrmaster; current vice-president and sales manager for J.H. Buhrmaster Comnpany, Inc.

James H. Buhrmaster (1968-present) -- Son of Louis and Margaret (Burch) Buhrmaster; current treasurer of J.H. Buhrmaster Company, Inc.

* * *

Being a person with the last name of Buhrmaster and trying to live something of a normal life in the village of Scotia must be a daunting task. Along with the celebrity and social status which is associated with being a Buhrmaster, there must also be tremendous pressure which comes along as the sharp side of the double-edged sword

With the family's history of service and dedication to the community being what it is, plus the family's incredible level of success and achievement almost out of sight for four generations now, any younger Buhrmaster must notice that bar has been set pretty high.

It might be frowned upon by the family elders if, say, one of the current young Buhrmaster descendants decided to drop out of high school and head for New York City in hopes of becoming a movie star or rock singer.

"I wouldn't say I ever felt any kind of pressure on me, or that just because I'm a Buhrmaster certain things are 'expected' of me," 40-year-old John Henry Buhrmaster said in the comfort of the first-floor office of his father, Louis Buhrmaster, at First National Bank of Scotia one humid mid-July morning.

"I was never pressured to assume a certain place in any of the family business, and I will be the same way with my (three) children. Right now I know they're up at Galway Lake running around the camp and enjoying the day, and later today I'll go up there and join them. When they grow up and get out on their own, as far as I'm concerned they can do whatever they want to do. I mean it."

John's proud father, 64-year-old Louis Henry Buhrmaster, nodded in agreement with the words his son had just uttered. Louis, president of the bank since 1969, echoed the sentiments of his son -- who is now also a key officer in the operation of the bank.

"We all (Buhrmasters) enjoy what we're doing. My grandfather (J.H.) worked here, my father, me and now John ... we try to let our children feel their way through it (family business) and see what they want to do, but I don't feel any of us were pressured into it," Louis said. "I know I didn't feel pressure. I just decided to go right into working for the family when I got out of the Army."

One constant throughout the family, however, is a sense of what the Buhrmaster ancestors accomplished to make the community a better place in which to live and work.
It is not something which they take lightly.

"My grandfather J.H., and Art Buhrmaster, were hard workers -- to begin with," Louis Buhrmaster said. "They started their farming and milking business on the site of what is now KAPL (Knolls Atomic Power Laboratory) in Niskayuna. Then they bought land on Sacandaga Road here in Scotia and settled the business and their homes here."

The business grew and grew and grew.

"They sold concrete to make streets and roads and sidewalks all the way up New York state to the Canadian border. They had sort of a monopoly on it," Louis said. "My grandfather didn't get into the fuel oil business right away, but eventually he did."

Louis and John Buhrmaster, father and son, listened with interest to the story related earlier by Tony Dorazio Sr. concerning J.H. Buhrmaster's kindness and generosity toward desperate customers, including his own father, during The Great Depression.

"Yes, my grandfather was that way," Louis said. "Especially during the Depression, when coal was in short supply, he made sure everyone got it who needed it. He'd tell them to come in and pay when they could. They'd sign a note in good faith and then pay when they could."

John Henry Buhrmaster might have aspired to high political office had it not been for family sadness. He was well on his way up the political ladder as member of the New York State Assembly from 1932 to 1936. But his two oldest sons, Neil and Louis, died of tuberculosis during his term. Louis, just 27, died in 1933. Neil, the eldest, died in 1936 at just 32 years of age.

"We think he just lost all interest in politics after that and decided to come home and stay home," Louis said. "But he had a strong work ethic he inherited from his father and mother, and he stayed very involved in everything -- his church, the businesses, and he even started a whole neighborhood of camps up in Galway Lake that were made up of all Scotia people. It's called Ruback's Grove; a lot of Scotia families found their way up there."

Louis Buhrmaster's desk in his First National office is adorned with many artificial turtles made of porcelain, colored glass, metal and wood. The tortoise seems a most ironic image for a prominent member of a family of fast-moving civic leaders. Or is it more of proof of the old adage that slow and sure wins the race?

Louis Buhrmaster smiled and nodded his head at the suggestion.

"I've just always had a fondness for turtles," he explained. "I like to have these artificial ones here on the desk here for when kids come in, so they can pick them up and hold them. I used to catch real turtles at Galway Lake when I was a boy. I'd go around with a net and get them off of logs when they were sunning themselves. I'd keep them as pets for awhile and then let them go. My mother hated them, especially one day in 1953 when I had some of them in boxes in the car and they all got loose!"

It is difficult to speculate on how different Scotia's history might have turned out had Christian Heinrich Buhrmaster not left Germany so many years ago to come to America. Suffice to say the village would not be the same had Buhrmaster decided to stay in his homeland.

"We (Buhrmaster family members) all sort of have an awareness of what needs to be done in the community," John Buhrmaster said. "A real wake-up call for me was when I was a young boy in October of 1971 and the village observed 'Kenneth L. Buhrmaster Week.' Before that, I wasn't really cognizant of what it meant to be a Buhrmaster."

Louis agreed.

"I feel very fortunate to have had the parents and grandparents that I've had," Louis said. "They gave me direction. They impressed on me that you can't just serve yourself and your own needs, but that you have to serve others -- and that's the way the world should work."

Part XI
Collins Park

Certain Irish eyes were smiling back in 1842 when Theodore W. Sanders sold the land (including the Abraham Glen House, which is now the Scotia Public Library) now known as Collins Park.

Those Irish eyes belonged to two lads from the old sod -- Charles and James Collins of Kilrea, Ireland, who bought the house and the land for $11,925. It was a 78-acre parcel of land. In all, the Collins brothers owned roughly 160 acres total -- much of which is now the village of Scotia.

Now you know, if you didn't know already, where Scotia got the name for Collins Park, Collins Lake, Collins Street. There even was an oldtime amateur baseball team that played at Collins Park's ball diamond, and the team was called the Jaycees (for J.C., or James Collins.)

When the last descendant of the Collins family (Miss Annie Collins, daughter of Charles) died in 1922, the village of Scotia acquired the land now known as Collins Park, including the Abraham Glen House. In a *Scotia Journal* article (July 21, 1976), former Scotia historian Donald A. Keefer stated that in 1928 "The Collins estate deeded the house and the land to the Village of Scotia for $30,000 stipulating that the land was

The legendary Abraham Glen House, now the public library, and adjoining buildings as this area of Collins Park looked around 1940.

This is how (top photo) Schonowee Avenue looked around 1915 as a horsedrawn carriage heads toward the old covered bridge leading to Schenectady. The Mohawk River is on the right, what is now Collins Park is on the left. In the bottom photo, taken in 1987 from a position further west on Mohawk Avenue, automobiles had long since replaced the horse and carriage, the train tracks are gone, the covered bridge removed and a new landmark -- Jumpin' Jacks outdoor eatery -- established on the right. (Larry Hart collection.)

to be used as a public park and that the name 'Collins' was to be the name of the park."

Ahhhhh ... Collins Park. Just as any other person who ever grew up in Scotia, I have so many, many memories -- 99 percent of them good ones -- associated with the park. Little League, Babe Ruth and high school JV baseball games and practices. Dances on summer nights on the tennis courts (they used to be called "block dances.")

How about fishing? I used to fish along the shoreline, sometimes over in the Washington Avenue side (a spot which over the years has gained a well-deserved reputation as a "Lovers' Lane!") Usually, though, as a kid, a young man and sometimes even now I fish mostly in the area behind the ballfield which once was the old swimming area and beach (sometime in the late 1960s, the swimming area and beach were moved to the current location.) What can you catch? Oh, sunfish, perch, bass, bullheads ... sometimes a big carp. I'll always remember fishing there one early October morning with a boyhood pal, Bob Little, when those carp would occasionally come charging out of the water and then crash back onto the surface. I had never seen such big fish in my young life!

Can you have lived in Scotia and not know about the fireworks display (usually sponsored in recent years by Mark Lansing, owner and proprietor of the ultra-popular Jumpin' Jacks outdoor eatery) on or about every July 4th? Or, how about sliding down one of the snow-covered Collins Park hills by the library? On any given winter day, those slopes and the parking lot are filled with eager kids and their parents (and sometimes the family pooch) enjoying a day of winter fun.

Many people I interviewed or simply chatted with in connection with this book zeroed in on Collins Park, Collins Lake, Jumpin' Jacks and the Mohawk River as one of their favorite memories -- if not THE favorite -- associated with growing up in this village or living in Scotia as an adult. The park is a year-round magnet for fun, electric with things to do all

171

day and evening long -- even if it's just a simple walk on a quiet weekday morning, alone or with your dog or a special friend.

Here's another thought/feeling which I have associated with Collins Park: in my fantasy life, everytime I hear an outdoor-recorded concert kind of song (by somebody like Phil Collins, Billy Joel or the Eagles) on a tape or on the radio while I'm driving in the car, I make believe while the song is on that I am a famous singer-songwriter and it is ME giving a free concert to 50,000 fans in my hometown at Collins Park some warm, summer evening and everyone is having a great time! I make believe that I am a multi-millionaire success of an entertainer and I am stopping home to entertain my hometown and neighboring fans for free, down in the bowl in back of the library. The Western Gateway Bridge is backed up with traffic all the way to Schenectady with people trying to get in to see and hear, and the TV cameras are there saying they've never seen anything like this crowd and wondering how will the police manage the traffic snarls afterward, etc., etc. Quite a fantasy, eh? Oh, well .... it's just a fantasy. (But if I were a famous entertainer, I really would do that! Honest! But ... I'm not a famous entertainer. More's the pity.)

Some friends of mine have fond thoughts concerning Collins Park, too. Read on:

* * *

There have long been tennis courts in Collins Park. Joan (Spencer) Szablewski remembers them being there as a teen-aged girl, even though she wasn't much of a tennis player.

"Myself and a few other girls ... we didn't play tennis, but we liked boys!" Szablewski said, smiling widely at the memory. "We used to walk up and down Mohawk Avenue carrying our tennis racquets. We never went to play tennis ... we just wanted to see which boys were around."

Besides baseball, basketball and tennis -- sports which are STILL played at Collins Park -- football once was played there.

172

Collins Park got a facelift when the lake was dredged and the entire park area cleaned up and improved during 1946 and 1947. The Abraham Glen House and adjoining buildings watch over the "mud bowl" below in bottom photo. (Larry Hart collection.)

Real, official, legitimate high school varsity football. Before the present high school field was laid out and used behind the current high school on Sacandaga Road, the Scotia Tartans played all their home games at Collins Park.

Paul Grippo remembers.

Grippo, who played varsity football for Scotia down on the old "bowl" field of Collins Park during the autumns of 1954, 1955 and 1956, remembers how special it was.

"Dick Rollins and Craig Hitchcock were our coaches in those days," Grippo recalled. "What fun it was! I still think about those Saturdays when I'm down at the park. We used to get suited up at the school, and then they'd bus us down to the park field for the game, and people used to honk their horns behind us and people would wave as we drove down Sacandaga Road and up Mohawk Avenue. The high school band would march down there around 11 o'clock before the game and played at our game. It was a wonderful time in my life."

* * *

Mark Lansing

Mark Lansing, who lived on Vley Road as a youngster and teen, started working at Jumpin' Jacks -- located on the banks of the Mohawk River along Schonowee Avenue -- as a teen-ager before graduating from Scotia High in 1963. The outdoor eating establishment was wildly popular back in the mid-1950s when it was owned by Jack Brennan -- a former employee at the old Empire Market on Mohawk Avenue. The food stand at that time was simply called "The Charcoal Pit," while the ice cream portion of the establishment was called "Twin Freeze."

Lansing went off to Paul Smith's College after his high school days had ended, but he returned to Scotia -- and Brennan's "gold mine" at Collins Park -- as a very young man. He's been there ever since, although the Scotia native now lives in Burnt Hills.

"I worked here for awhile for Jack, but then I leased it from 1976 until 1989 when I bought Jack out," Lansing said one drizzly April afternoon in the snug comfort of his tiny office in the back of the ice cream store portion of his business.

Brennan, incidentally, died three years ago, according to Lansing. Brennan had lived in Florida in the latter part of his life.

A modest man in many ways, Lansing never saw the need to change the name of the popular spot -- which opens annually in late March or early April and closes Labor day weekend. It is open every day (except Easter Sunday) from 11 a.m. until about 11 p.m. Indeed, the name Jumpin' Jacks is derived from Brennan. The sign over the business depicts a jack-in-the-box clown popping out of a box, and the box reflects the initials JB for John Brennan. Lansing smiled and shook his head in a negative fashion when asked if he has ever considered changing the name to Lansingland or Mark's Place, or something similar.

"That would be foolish to change the name. People all around the Capital Region, I'm proud to say, know about Jumpin' Jacks. We have a pretty wide geographic radius we draw from," Lansing said.

Lansing has kept not only the name -- but the products which his ice cream and food counters offer -- almost exactly the same as they were in the 1950s when Brennan ran the business. If you buy a cheeseburger, hot dog, onion rings or ice cream cone there today, those items will taste the same way as you remember them from the 1950s.

"I just try to keep things the same. Why change it? If something's not broken, don't fix it," Lansing said. "Another thing that's the same is the people who work for me. There are about 25 to 30 employees here each season, and many of them are returning workers. Some of them have been with me a long time."

The employees know how to make the burgers and dogs (and steak sandwiches, fries, onion rings, fish sandwiches) just the way the public has come to know and enjoy them for over five decades.

"I don't know if there's a special secret to our burgers and hot dogs," Lansing said when pressed for details about his staff's work at the grill. "All our rolls are fresh from Freihofer's; we use White Eagle hot dogs, and we get our hamburger from Meatland in Broadalbin. We've actually gone through several meat outlets for the hamburger over the years, but the constant is that we have always used fresh meat that we keep refrigerated -- as opposed to frozen meat. If there's a secret, I think that's probably it. It's the same thing where if you buy a nice steak in a store and you cook it that same day or evening, it always tastes better than it will if you go home and put it in the freezer and eat it another day. It's true; trust me on that one."

The most hectic -- but also the most enjoyable and profitable -- day/evening of the season for Lansing and his staff is the date each year when Jumpin' Jacks holds its fireworks display at

You have to wait in a long line for a treat at Jumpin' Jacks on a normal summer day, but any longtime customer will agree -- it's always worth it! On this particular spring morning, however, the wait for a burger or hot dog was a short one. (Alan Hart photo.)

176

dusk. Lansing smiled, sat back in his chair and let out a knowing sigh when asked about the volume of trade his business does that day and evening. Literally thousands of people, after all, swarm to Collins Park that evening to roll out a blanket or set up folding chairs to see the annual show. (Many of them, obviously, make it a point to get a burger and fries or an ice cream cone as part of the trip.)

"It's a fun day, and I think it's a great goodwill-builder for us. I enjoy it," Lansing said. "I have no idea how much the single-day profit is for that date, but there is a limit. There's only so much food you can cook per hour. If you exceed that, your quality starts going the wrong way, and I'm not about to let that happen."

Lansing said that never, as a high-schooler working for Brennan, did he dream that someday he would own the business at all, let alone watch it grow into the true landmark of Scotia which it has become. He does not take that status for granted.

"Scotia is a special place ... that's for sure. It's a nice place to live. I don't live here anymore, but Scotia basically has never changed in the sense that you can walk almost anywhere in the village and not worry."

If there is one complaint which Lansing has heard about Jumpin' Jacks over the years, it's that customers wish he would stay open through the month of September and not close Labor Day weekend. He understands this point of view, but he has a good reason why he locks up in September.

"People around here are all burgered out by Labor Day," Lansing said. "By that, I mean people have been barbecuing all summer or eating down here, and they're starting to get a little tired of it. Besides that, the schools are opening up and the family unit is restored -- people do things as a family again after spending the summer doing separate things. Sure, we could do a business down here in September, but not the kind of volume you really need to stay open. That's why we close when we do."

Say, this author suddenly feels the craving for a big, fat cheeseburger with some fries. How about you?

Part XII
It's a Gas!

Everyone loves getting into his or her car and taking a drive ... either for a short distance or a long trip. In order to do that, of course, one has to keep doing something important -- keep putting gas into the vehicle.

Ever since Grundhoeffer's Drug Store at 208 Mohawk Avenue was in existence, drivers have been able to fill up in Scotia.

"It (drug store) had the first gas pump in Scotia," according to a letter to the editor in the *Scotia Journal* of Sept. 29, 1976, by Cerds H. Grundhoeffer. "I remember it well as I pumped thousands of gallons of gas from it."

Grundhoeffer wrote that Charles Steinmetz, the brilliant Schenectady scientist, was a regular customer at the store. He used to stop to purchase raspberry syrup.

"It was a favorite of Dr. Steinmetz's," she wrote. "He would often stop with his electric runabout on his way to his camp along the Mohawk River."

But when I think of gas stations located in Scotia during the 1950s and 1960s, two come to mind right away -- Arkley Tire Company, a Shell station, on the corner of Mohawk and Collins Street, and Montana's, a Sunoco station a block further west on the corner of Mohawk and Ballston Avenue. By sheer coincidence, I guess, those owners -- Arkley Mastro Sr. and Dominic Montana -- both happened to have sons my age, and I eventually became good friends with both of them: Arkley Mastro Jr. and Donnie Montana.

I first met Arkley Mastro Jr. when we were both fourth-graders at Sacandaga School in the 1950s. My first impression of Mastro was that he was a big, tall quiet kid who seemed like a really nice fellow. The other impression I had of him, right off the bat, was that I thought he looked a lot like a young Ricky Nelson. (For all you younger readers out there, Ricky -- in later years,

In the early 1940s, the corner of Mohawk Avenue and Ballston Avenue looked like this. Note street signs/arrows in lower right corner informing travelers that Utica is west, Saratoga north. Below, in a 1987 photograph, Dominic Montana's Sunoco station had long since replaced the aging building shown in the top photo. (Larry Hart collection.)

Rick -- Nelson was a 1950s rock and roll star and the youngest son of real-life TV husband and wife Ozzie and Harriet Nelson.)

Early on in our friendship, I learned that his father -- Arkley Sr. -- owned the Shell station on Mohawk Avenue and Collins Street, the one my mom and dad used to take our cars to. Arkley and I became fast friends right away. We just hit it off for some reason, and who knows why that happens? It just happens. Maybe because we both liked playing sports, both were interested in the same girls (!) and just seemed to enjoy each other's company and talking and doing things.

Mastro has, in fact, been a lifetime friend who has reappeared in my life at critical junctions ... not constant from Day One on to today in 2004 but rather in and out at crucial moments. We were strong friends right through elementary, junior high and high school. We launched play rockets in a field near his home, played sports together as teammates and opponents, visited each other's homes. (As mentioned in an earlier chapter, we played in the same starting lineup on the first Scotia High soccer team in 1963.)

He didn't play varsity basketball on that juggernaut team Scotia had that year (1963-64) which won the Section II Class A title. He sure could have helped, because he was good ... good enough to go on to become a standout player as a collegian at Clarkson. Not bad, eh?

Some years passed and I lost touch with him for awhile, but once again we found ourselves together again as members of the 109th Tactical Airlift Group -- the Glenville-based unit of the New York State Air National Guard -- from 1968 through 1974. He was an administrations officer while I was a sergeant in the Base Equipment Management Office. We saw a lot of each other in those years -- once a month on a weekend, anyway.
Mastro also stood by me as an attorney at a time in my life when I really needed an old friend to help me through a tough time. As always, he was there.

Another fellow I saw during those years in the Air National Guard was Don Montana. I hadn't gotten to know Don as well

Don Montana and Arkley Mastro Jr., both sons of noted automotive station owners a block apart in Scotia during their respective youth and young adulthood, both have fond memories of this luncheonette (also known as Schuyler's Restaurant at one time.) Both their fathers often ate and conversed with each other along with other friends and businessmen there. (Larry Hart collection.)

as Arkley (he attended school from eighth grade on at Christian Brothers Academy in Albany) except to say "Hello," but we got to be good friends when we went to basic training together in June and July of 1968 at Lackland Air Force Base in San Antonio, Tex. Don, myself and Hank Mancini of Amsterdam were the only three guys from New York State in our squadron housed in Dorm 6339 under Sgt. Henry Onacki.

Don Montana was one of our squad leaders. Me? I wasn't a leader, but I think I was a pretty good follower. I did what my Uncle Norman Hart, himself a former Guardsman, had advised me to do down there: Norm had warned me, "Keep your eyes and ears open and your mouth shut, and you'll be OK." (It proved to be darn good advice.)

After we both served in the Air Guards, Montana seemed to vanish off the face of the earth. I never knew what happened to him until I began working on this volume.

Unlike the Mastro station (Arkley Tire Company), which went out of business in August of 1981 after a 35-year run, Montana's station is still a visible landmark business in Scotia. Arkley Mastro Sr. and Dom Montana have both passed away, but they each made an indelible impression in the minds and lives of Scotians during the 1950s, 1960s and beyond. Montana's station is now strictly a car repair business, operated by Gene Conover. (Conover said in an April visit to the station that he stopped selling gas in 1999.)

Arkley Mastro lives in Glenville with his wife, Florence, and their nine-year-old son, Kevin.

Don Montana makes his home in Fairfield, Conn., with his wife, the former Bonnie Frasier, but they also spend many weekends of the year at their property in Lake George. Their two daughters -- Alendre and Lara -- are grown. Montana, who worked for many years for General Electric and Aetna Insurance, is now head of human resources for A&P in Fairfield.

Both sons of perhaps the two most successful service station owners in Scotia during the 1950s and 1960s have certainly made names for themselves in their own right as adults. It was nice to catch up with both of these old friends to get their views on what their growing years were like in "Dear Old Scotia."

Here's what each had to say in separate interviews:

* * *

Arkley Mastro Jr. knows his first name is rather unique. If you don't think so, then try to find someone else in the world with that name. I bet you'll have a difficult time.

"I'm named after my father, of course, and my (paternal) grandmother gave my father the name 'Arkley' after a 300-year-old village in northern England. It's a tiny little village about 40 miles north of London," Mastro explained during a late-June interview in a Latham restaurant near his law firm. "In 1977, about three years after Dad died, I went to England with my brother, Jeff. Part of the reason I went was because I wanted to finally see this place I was named after. I took a double-decker red bus from London as far as it would go, then hired a taxi. I told him I wanted to go to Arkley, and the cabby looked at me and said, 'What for?' I showed him my business card and told him I was named after the village. Well, he started driving toward where he thought Arkley was, but he had to keep stopping and asking directions. People would ask why we were headed there and the cabby would say, 'Because the bloke inside wants to see it ... he's named after the village!' "

Finally, Mastro arrived at his destination.

"There was this old, old tavern there -- probably as old as the town -- and it had a sign outside," Mastro said. "It was a huge sign with a depiction of Noah, the ark, and two of many kinds of animals boarding the ark. That's when I knew we were in the right place."

Speaking of communities, Mastro has a great fondness for the city of Boston, but his roots reach deeply into Scotia-Glenville earth. He has great respect for his hometown and its people.

So did his father, Arkley Mastro Sr.

"My father was a great manager; a great organizer. He knew how to run a business and how to treat people -- customers and employees -- with fairness and respect," Mastro said. "Dad worked very hard, too. He used to work basically from seven in the morning until 11 at night. He always told me and my brothers, Jeff and Tim, that he didn't want the same thing for us ... he wanted us to go to college and law school so we didn't have to work as hard as he did. He discouraged us from wanting to be part of the family business."

Fate, however, pulled Mastro into the center of the picture .... out of necessity.

"I was in my first year of law school when we learned Dad had cancer," Mastro said. "For awhile, it looked like he had beaten it, but it came back three or four years later, and he died. I was an attorney in Boston at the time, but I resigned that position and came home to handle Dad's estate for my mother, and I took over Dad's tire company as president -- with the idea that I'd hold onto it until we knew if Jeff or Tim wanted to run it. But Tim went to medical school and Jeff went into banking, so we sold it to Johnny Antonelli -- the former New York Giants pitcher who had a franchise of stores."

Mastro remembers not only how hard his father worked, but also how much his father enjoyed other people -- even his keenest rival, Dominic Montana.

"Dad and Mr. Montana were pretty good friends, even though they obviously were competitors," Mastro said. "Do you remember the gasoline price wars of the 1960s? Prices were going down and there was competition for customers. Dad used to see Mr. Montana in the luncheonette in the morning and they'd talk about the price of gas. My father might say, for instance, that he was charging 18 cents a gallon. Mr. Montana would respond, 'Yes, I'm charging 18 cents, too.' Then Dad would leave and after awhile he'd walk out on the corner and look down the street and he'd see that Mr. Montana had lowered his price to 17.9, so Dad would then lower HIS price to 16.9! It was kind of the gasoline price war that was going on all over the country -- right there in Scotia in microcosm."

* * *

It was a simple question: why has Montana's service station been such a successful, longtime landmark of Scotia -- one that has lasted into its seventh decade -- whereas most other businesses in the village have not had that same kind of staying power?

Don Montana, in a telephone interview one June evening from Connecticut, perhaps with good reason was unable to offer a simple explanation for the reasons for the longevity of his father's enterprise.

"It's a lot of things, I think," Montana said. "First, I think you have to look at the location: Mohawk Avenue and Ballston Avenue. I mean, it's perfect -- the junction of two of the village's main arteries. As a result, he used to sell a lot of gas! It was the highest-producing station for pumping Sunoco gas in the entire area ... for a long time."

But location was not the lone reason Dominic Montana was so successful in putting deep roots into that station -- roots which last to this day.

"Dad was very sincere about offering customer service. My father was a really good man. I say that with all honesty ... not just because I'm his son," Montana said. "Remember the gas crunch of the early 1970s? Dad would sell 3,000 gallons of gas a day by noontime and he would have to close down, by law. But I can tell you this ... he used to take care of special customers; elderly people who had been with him a long time. But he also took care of new customers who were, you know, kind of panicky. People told me after the crisis was over, 'You know, your Dad was wiping windows and taking care of us and not rushing us through acting like we were lucky to be getting gas from him.' I was very proud of my father for that. I've always remembered those comments. It shows the kind of man he was. And that's not all: that station was a success because my father was a very astute man. He started a couple of gas stations during World War II in Niskayuna and Schenectady, before he started the current business on Mohawk Avenue. He also had a job as a toolmaker at GE, and he got into buying and selling property and making a profit. He had a sound eye for real estate and what it was worth and its possibilities, he could foresee when a road might come through that a certain property would be worth more ... he was doing all that while he was running the station, too. I think Dad was a really bright guy."

Indeed. And a man with a sense of humor, as well.

"Dad loved to pull practical jokes," Montana said. "He used to go around the village and put up 'For sale' signs on the front lawns of certain friends of his. Things like that. He loved visiting with people -- customers and other businessmen. I remember he used to go to lunch as often as he could with other businessmen in his area like Botsy Slover, Tom Swire, Dud Rowledge ... and other guys. They all used to go across the street to Schuyler's Restaurant and eat lunch and talk about everything. I remember coming home from college in the winter. I'd be pumping gas for Dad and freezing my behind off, and I'd see him sitting in the window of Schuyler's waving at me!"

Don Montana, one of four children in his family, went to Villanova University. He is still grateful for the opportunities which his father and mother -- both now deceased -- gave him in life.

"My mom died when I was still pretty young. Dad died in 1996 at the Baptist home there in Scotia. But actually, I was lucky to have him around as long as I did. He got hit by a car -- accidentally -- crossing the avenue one day in the 1970s. He was on his way over to Gibbons and Burke (law firm) across the street, and a driver slowed and stopped to let him by, but someone else in the other lane didn't see him and struck him. He was rushed to the hospital and we almost lost him, but he recovered. But Dad was different after that; he was never quite the same."

Part XIII
Memories

My late teen years living in Scotia were punctuated by three significant incidents which occurred in late fall, early winter -- each one year apart. The first was the most memorable and one which deeply impacted American and world history. It was the assassination of President John F. Kennedy on Nov. 22, 1963.

The succeeding two were much less significant but just as memorable and certainly altered forever the way I had previously taken for granted things like a warm house, electricity and lights. I'm talking about the Ice Storm of 1964, which occurred the first weekend of December, and the Blackout of 1965, when power in the whole Northeast corridor went out one weekday evening in early November.

The Ice Storm came suddenly and wreaked furious havoc in Scotia and all over upper New York State, as sleet began falling in mid-afternoon and soon caked inches of thick, heavy ice on tree limbs everywhere. Limbs fell on power lines and pulled down live wires, knocking out power and exposing dangerous live wires on nearly every block. Seemingly all over the Northeast, homes lost their power around 5 or 6 p.m., and some of us in Scotia were without power for a week or so. The lucky ones had natural gas with which to cook and water with which to drink and wash

Scenes like this one, with thick coats of ice on downed tree limbs -- often with power lines under them -- were common all over the streets of the village of Scotia during the infamous "Ice Storm" in early December of 1964. (Larry Hart photo.)

187

ourselves and utensils. We learned to use candles to do things like read books and play board games.

I remember awakening that next morning in our Sanders Avenue home to the sound of Niagara Mohawk workers warning us with their bullhorns, "Please stay in your homes" because they were working with chain saws to clear the street and trying to restore power. We heard the whine of chain saws for days.

Longtime Scotia barber Vern Foster remembers the Ice Storm of '64 very well. He was cutting a customer's hair at his barber shop on Mohawk Avenue when, suddenly, the power went out.

"We wondered what the heck was going on. I had two other customers waiting, and one of them got up and went to the window and looked across the street to the power pole in front of the Turf. He said, 'It's probably the transformer over there across the street.' Little did any of us know it had happened all over the area, and we were without power about a week, weren't we?"

Bucky Dorazio, too, recalls the storm.

"Chain saws ... trees down all over the place ... no power in our house; sure, I remember," Dorazio said. "You know, the next day was a Saturday, and my sister Sandy had to go to the wedding of a friend -- Patty Pink -- that day at a church out on Bolt Road. They still had the wedding anyway, even without power and with all the other obvious problems created by the storm."

The scene was similar -- except for the absence of chain saws -- a year later with the famous Blackout.

Somewhere, the power grid for the whole Northeast was short-circuited, plunging our part of the country into darkness for a few days. I remember riding home in a car with next-door neighbor Bill Vazal. We both were students at Hudson Valley Communiuty College in Troy at the time. We were coming across the Western Gateway Bridge about 5 p.m., wondering why our village was in utter darkness at such an hour. It was bizarre; like something out of a science-fiction movie. (Oddly, the situation was repeated on Aug. 14, 2003, but since on this more recent occasion it was during warmer weather, and power was more quickly restored, history may not remember that evening in quite the same way as the Blackout of '65.)

The "Blackout of '65" occurred near dusk one early November evening in 1965, necessitating that citizens of the northeast, accustomed to their comforts, temporarily had to learn how to cope without electricity and instead use candles for light. This scene of State Street in downtown Schenectady was taken from the second floor of the old Schenectady Gazette building near the railroad bridge. (Larry Hart photo.)

Both the Ice Storm and the Blackout served to remind us all that one should not take things things like warmth and electricity for granted ... ever again.

Sharon (Hartley) Dunlap remembers spending that unlit evening of the Blackout of '65 talking on the telephone ... all night.

"My boyfriend at the time -- John Engel -- was interning somewhere in New York City," Dunlap said. "It was weird because I was eating dinner that night with my family and suddenly the lights dimmed and then went out altogether. After awhile, John called to talk, and I stayed on the phone talking to him the whole night. Hey, there was nothing else to do!"

Much more vivid in my own mind, and I'm sure in the mind of anyone else who remembers Nov. 22, 1963, was JFK's assassination and the days which followed. It occurred in the afternoon -- during the last Scotia High school period of the day that Friday. Myself, I was seated in the auditorium along with all the other members of the high school chorus. For some reason, we were practicing for the upcoming Thanksgiving assembly concert, but we were in the seats and not on the stage. Maybe halfway through the class, Mr. Henry Sullivan, who was our conductor, was interrupted by Mr. Carl Steubing, who walked out to whisper something meant for Sullivan's ears only. Mr. Sullivan then informed us that the president had been shot by an assassin in Dallas, and a collective gasp went up from us all. He was still alive, we were told, but obviously it did not look good. We continued to practice the traditional holiday hymn, "We Gather Together," but in a few minutes Mr. Steubing returned to give Mr. Sullivan a sad update: our president was dead.

We were stunned.

Me? What I remember most of that whole rest of the weekend was that I didn't know what I was supposed to do. It didn't seem right to stay home and watch the television. I thought, "I should do something." But what? It also didn't seem right to go out and do anything. (It was a feeling repeated on Sept. 11, 2001 when terrorists attacked the Twin Towers in New York, the Pentagon in Washington, D.C., and threatened to attack another target before the attempt was aborted by brave heroes who rushed the attackers and forced a plane crash in a field in Pennsylvania.)

What did I do that night of Nov. 22, 1963? I played basketball, that's what. I know, it sounds insensitive and I don't know why I did it, but I did. I remember coming home and calling Russ Hawkins to ask if our scheduled Methodist Church team scrimmage against Scotia Reformed at Sacandaga School was still "on" that night as scheduled. Russ asked his dad and our coach, Ken Hawkins Sr. The answer was that, yes, it was still on ... because the feeling was we couldn't do anything about what had happened, anyway, and it might be best to have life go on as usual as best we all could. I felt funny about it, but I went to the scrimmage and, if it isn't too insensitive to say it, I had a pretty darn good game, even though we lost. I shot 6-for-9 from the floor and scored 12 points. (For me, that was very good!) It's odd how you remember something unimportant like that against the background of something so historic by comparison. Maybe it was because I truthfully did not feel like playing that night, so I just relaxed and played well. Oddest of all is that since that day, whenever people have asked me what I was doing the day Kennedy was shot, I tell them I went out and played basketball that night, and the people think that was a crazy thing to do. Maybe it was. Yes ... I'm sure it was. But please understand ... we didn't know what to do. We were all aimless that day; every American was.

Then I remember watching on TV as the people filed past the president's coffin lying in state at the rotunda of the Capitol in Washington, D.C., and the single white horse pulling the carriage with JFK's coffin down Constitution Avenue to Arlington National Cemetery for burial, all to the macabre beat of a single drum.

And there was the sombre, chilling sermon given by then-pastor Rev. Robert Van Court -- a minister I very much admired -- that following Sunday morning at the First Baptist Church, followed by the bizarre shooting (on live TV) of Lee Harvey Oswald, Kennedy's own assassin, by Jack Ruby. No one who experienced those compelling, historic days of 1963 will ever forget the events of that weekend.

OK, enough of that. These were all sad or trying memories of growing up in Scotia. But what's my favorite memory of being a kid or a teen-ager in this village? Hey, I'm glad you asked. Of course, this whole book has been an attempt to tell you what I thought it was like to live here in the 1950s and 1960s as a kid and teen.

Forced to choose one single, solitary favorite memory of Scotia, however, I would say this: I don't know what exact date it is, but ... I'm on my bicycle and I am a happy 11 or 12-year-old heading off to practice with my Kiwanis baseball team of the Scotia Little League at Collins Park on a sunny, warm Saturday morning about 8:30 a.m. I've got my own Adirondack bat and my own Rawlings "Sam Mele Model" glove (both of which Mom and Dad had bought me when I made the team) slung over the handlebars of my bike, and I'm pedalling down Sanders Avenue, up South Ten Broeck Street, and down Glen Avenue, eagerly looking forward to seeing the other guys and playing ball. I was very, very proud to be a member of that team and to wear that red and white Kiwanis cap. I wore it everywhere, all the time, taking it off only in church, restaurants and to go to sleep. (Sudden thought: I wish I still had that thing. Why did I ever throw it away?)

On the way down Glen Avenue, I cut through the grocery store parking lot and I pass by the Hometown Bakery, and I can smell something wonderful baking. Mmmmmmm!

This is a memory that was repeated over and over. It was a great time, and I look back now and I see how lucky I was to be able to enjoy something (playing ball) I loved so much, to live in a safe and caring environment and surrounded with so much happiness and love of family and friends in a great little village of our country.

OK. This is it for me, now. I've truly enjoyed writing this book and getting reacquainted with so many of the people you have heard about -- and from -- in the pages which have preceded. I now turn it over to others to reach the finish line by giving you THEIR favorite memories of Scotia. I asked many people who had a part in the making of this book for their own favorite memories of Scotia. Most of the people responded with an answer.

Here is what they said, with the persons listed in alphabetical order:

* * *

Fred "Corky" Bleser Jr. -- "Favorite memory? I guess just growing up in Scotia itself is my favorite memory. Everybody kind of hung out together; everybody knew one another and there were always good times whenever you did -- right on through high school. It was a lot of fun to grow up in Scotia. I live in Burnt Hills now, but I still go into Scotia, and it's been quite a few years, now, since I lived there. But it's pretty much the same place. Everybody knows you."

John Buhrmaster -- "For me, it was the bicentennial celebration of 1976. We had just finished the creation of Freedom Park, and I spent a lot of time down there. I remember the barge display, the fireworks, all the people ... that's when I really got a sense of my roots and how lucky I was to be living right here, right now."

Louis Buhrmaster -- "My favorite memory was 1971 when Scotia had 'Kenneth Buhrmaster week' in honor of my father. I always had known what he had done for the community, but that was when I first realized how much everyone appreciated him and all the things he had done. I'll never forget that."

Annie (Hart) Clary -- "I have so many memories, really. But I guess the thing I remember most fondly is going to Jumpin' Jacks and having burgers, fries and ice cream together with my family. It was always very special."

Tony "Bucky" Dorazio Jr. -- "If I can classify a favorite memory of Scotia as an entire year, I'd have to say it was my senior year of high school. I really enjoyed it, and it was more fun than any I ever had. I even enjoyed that one year more than my four years of college at Oswego. To pick one single favorite memory, though, it would be running over to the high school in 1961, 1962 when I was 10 or 11 and riding on the snow plow whenever we had a bad snowstorm. Dayton Preddice and Don Petersen, who were maintenance men at the high school, used to let me sit in the truck right between them. You know, I believe winters were a lot more harsh in those days. We used to get some really snowy winters."

Vern Foster -- "My favorite memory of Scotia probably is playing in the annual Scotia-Glenville Golf Tournament for many years. You'd get out on the golf course for what we called the 'Scotia Open' and you'd see people you knew from businesses and other places who were never on the course, and it was a very nice day every year. You had to either live in Scotia or be working in Scotia in order to qualify."

Paul Grippo -- "I say with great pride that I played in the Scotia Little League the first year it was formed, and I was a member of the very first Scotia Little League all-star team -- in 1951. I played for American Legion, and my manager was Jim Gersbach. But when it came to the all-stars, the manager was Rotary manager Tick Turnbull, and he was a no-nonsense guy and a tough, old bird. If you can believe this, he used to demand that we kids stayed in our cellars on days that we had games. He wanted us to stay cool as could be and save our strength and stamina for the game. We went over to Rotterdam and beat those guys pretty good, but then we had to go play Schenectady with that manager, Mike Maietta. Schenectady really whaled on us. But playing on that all-star team is my favorite memory of Scotia."

Mary (Kelefant, Westad) Hart's favorite memory of her childhood in Scotia is the times she would dress up in adult clothes with her good friend and across-the-street neighbor, Wendy Swartz, and push their dolls in carriages around neighborhood streets. (Photo courtesy of Mary Kelefant.)

Mary Carol (Kelefant, Westad) Hart -- "I always remember being around five years old when Wendy (Swartz) Near, my friend across the street, and I would dress up in women's clothes and put our dollies in strollers and walk around the whole block of Albermarle, Meriline and Neal Streets. It was a different time then; our society was different. We felt very safe doing that, and our mothers felt safe with us doing that because no harm would come to us."

Mary (Sturdy) Kelefant -- "I liked to walk over to hear the fife and drum brigade practice on the roof of Mohawk School. We lived on

194

Glen Avenue -- a block away from the school -- when I was a child, and we'd hear them practicing. The men would put ladders up against the walls of the school and go up on the rooftop to play. All the Millard boys played in the brigade. I also have always enjoyed the fireworks, too, down in the (Collins) park. They shoot them off by the riverside now, but they used to have it in back of the library."

Jennifer (Hart) Lepel -- "Probably my fondest memory of Scotia is going to the Scotia Cinema for movies with my family. I remember seeing a whole bunch of movies there, including one of the Muppet ones. And can I add a couple of close seconds? I also loved going to the Fourth of July fireworks and the Memorial Day parade on Mohawk Avenue. I tell myself I go nowadays because my mother likes to go to those things -- she never misses them. But I confess that I like to go, too."

Rachael (Hart) Mason -- "That's so hard to answer; I have so many favorite childhood memories, especially of Scotia. I guess one big one is going to the Scotia Library. I always loved that little children's room in the back. Then there was that store (Swire's) with the wooden floors that my father used to take us to near the Scotia Theater. When you talk about strictly school memories, I always loved the Halloween parades at our school -- Sacandaga

Scotia's annual Memorial Day parade is one of the favorite memories many villagers have of the years in which they have lived in Scotia. In this photo taken at the parade in 1947 near the intersection of Mohawk Avenue and Ballston Avenue, a fife and drum brigade performs for the crowd. (Larry Hart photo.)

School -- when we'd march around the neighborhood streets in our costumes. And I really liked going to the Scotia Diner on Mohawk Avenue with Grandma (Arlette) Merz. She used to take me and my sisters in there for pie."

Arkley Mastro Jr. -- "Scotia was such a great place in which to grow up. There were stores, the Scotia Theater, ice cream stores like Riverside Dairy down on Ten Broeck Street as well as that Stewart's on Mohawk Avenue where you could make your own sundae! Really, Scotia was pretty self-contained; there were places to get anything you wanted. And if you wanted to, you could walk or ride over to Schenectady ... 'Overtown,' we used to call it. But I guess my favorite single memory of Scotia is the 1954 celebration at Collins Park. I remember all the big Ferris wheels and being in awe of them."

Roy Matthews -- "My favorite memory is probably one of the many times I went down to the park when I was a kid or teen-ager. It used to be fun to play games down there and then wander over to the Twin-Freeze for ice cream. They used to have carnivals in the park, too, and they were a lot of fun."

Ed McNally -- "There was that whole experience of being a little kid growing up on Glen Avenue and doing things up and down the block, on Wyman Street and Sanders Avenue with the Mohawk School playground. I remember that's how I learned to ride a two-wheel bike; one day I just took my bike out on quiet little Wyman Street and kept at it until I learned to ride the darn thing. I have another special memory of Scotia: how about Mondy's Delicatessen? He (owner) was really nice to me. I used to walk up to the back door and bang on the door and he'd give me a free doughnut, even though he knew my mom (Bonnie Munro) didn't approve. She'd always know, though, because I'd go home and have sugar or frosting on my face!"

Albert Moser Sr. -- "The second year we lived here -- 1954 -- Scotia was celebrating its sesquicentennial, and that has to be my favorite memory of living in this village. Back then there was a big parade and big doings at Collins Park. I played in a dance band there, and there was a big concert. And all the men had to grow a beard and mustache -- they called it 'The Brothers of the Brush' -- or they'd throw you in jail. They passed out wooden nickels, and there were fireworks and a carnival at the park. It was a good time!"

Peg Moser -- "I'll always think of going to Jumpin' Jacks as my favorite memory of Scotia. Back in the early days, before it was called Jumpin' Jacks even, they had a little train down there that ran around the parking lot. To this day, anytime our boys come home

Albert and Peg Moser, longtime Scotians who are natives of Pennsylvania, both have favorite memories of their half century of life in Scotia. (Larry Hart photo.)

to visit, we have to go down to Jumpin' Jacks. It will be the last day of a visit and I'll ask them if there's something they want to do that we haven't yet done, and they'll say, 'Can we go down to Jumpin' Jacks for supper?' "

Bonnie (Hart) Munro -- "That's easy -- going down as a teen-ager with my family once a week or so during the summer to 'The Charcoal Pit' for cheeseburgers and onion rings and fries, then getting ice cream at the Twin Freeze. It's called Jumpin' Jacks now. It was a real treat each time, and you could watch the water skiers working out or having a water ski show, too."

Catherine Ritchey -- "No single favorite memory except to say my favorite memory is the people of Scotia themselves. I work at the Baptist Health, Nursing and Rehabilitation Center, and you can't believe the number of people who come in here now

197

as a patient or are admitting a parent, and these are people I came to know when my husband and I were operating the Scotia Theater. And I think the beauty of Scotia is you have the charm of the small town, but you're connected to so many places -- the Adirondacks, New York City, Cape Cod ... all a few hours drive. I've always loved that connection."

Paul Ritchey -- "Favorite memory of Scotia? I'd have to say it was in the 1950s when I worked for my father at the Scotia Theater. It was an awful lot of fun to be there in those times. One of my jobs was to change the marquee outside, and sometimes it was in the dead of winter and late at night on that rickety, old ladder. I'll tell you what, too: I wish I still had a lot of those old movie posters that I threw away in those years. They'd be worth a fortune."

Tim Sawicki -- "I grew up in West Glenville and didn't get to Scotia very much as a child or teen-ager except for school, but my favorite memory of Scotia was back in 1976 when Freedom Park

Joan (Spencer) Szablewski, currently Glenville's town historian, has many favorite memories of having lived in Scotia. Some of the best include her long friendships with childhood buddies Bob Metzger (center) and Charlie Pastore. This photograph was taken on the porch steps at 132 Vley Road when they were all about 5 years old. (Photo courtesy of Joan Szablewski.)

opened alongside Jumpin' Jacks by the Mohawk River. I sang and played guitar on that flat stage with some of my high school friends there at Freedom Park right after it opened. That was a very proud moment for me, and I'll never forget it."

Joan (Spencer) Szablewski -- "My favorite memory is probably the many friends I grew up with here in Scotia. A few years ago I went to a high school reunion and I saw Bob Metzger and Charlie Pastore -- two great friends from my childhood and school years -- and I hadn't seen them in about 40 years. Charlie made me a music box after that reunion and sent it to me, and his wife told me that he had made just a few of them for people who were very special in his life so that they would remember him. He died a short time after that, so I treasure that music box."

Lifetime Scotian Bill Vazal, now 57, of all his many memories of Scotia remembers most his many visits to Collins Park as a child. (Alan Hart photo.)

Bill Vazal -- "For me, my favorite childhood memory of Scotia, hands down, is just getting on my bike and going to Collins Park to do something. My grandmother and my father never minded where I went as long as I told them where I was going. There was so much to do at Collins Park. Of course, there was a lot to do right across the street from my house at Mohawk School! When I was little, I used to go go over to the school playground and watch my older brother Frank play baseball or basketball, and then I got older and played sports there myself. And then, when I got even older, there was that 'tunnel of love' where you'd go in and kiss the girls. It was just a cement circle, but we called it the 'tunnel of love.' "

Katharine Jean "K.J." (Kelefant, Jones) Walters -- "My favorite single-day memory of Scotia is probably the day I was sitting in class in school and they moved that entire house off of Sacandaga Road. It was a strange sight to see a house being transported down the street. The teacher stopped the class so we could all watch it. My favorite memory of something that happened more than once is probably flying kites on the Lincoln School playground near my home on Albermarle."

George Westad -- "Probably my favorite memory of growing up in Scotia is the many days my grandmother, Kiku Westad, took me to Collins Park. She'd watch me swim in the lake and then we used to go over to Jumpin' Jacks for food."

Index

203

A REMEMBRANCE OF MY
"TALES OF OLD DORP"

By LARRY HART

Introduction

It was early in the afternoon on February 14th, 2004 ... the sad day of the wake and funeral of my beloved father, Larry Hart. The immediate family was gathering at Mom and Dad's home on Droms Road in Glenville in order to depart together for the demanding events which lay ahead.

Just as I got to the house, my sister -- Bonnie Munro of New Scotland -- met me at the stairway holding something in an 8 x 10 envelope. She said, "Alan, I have something here I think you should look at. I'm not sure what to do with it."

I opened the envelope and saw the contents inside. I wasn't sure what to do with it, either, but I certainly knew what it was: it was a manuscript of Dad's ... the beginning of what would have been his 15th book about local history!

Bonnie and I talked about it very briefly. Dad had begun the work about four years earlier, only because we in the immediate family were prodding him to do so. Dad was beginning to show the telltale signs of Alzheimer's Disease, and as anyone would expect, he was very self-conscious about it. He knew he was beginning to forget things; how to spell words, what things were called. (For example, if you asked him in 2000 to go find a screwdriver in his tool box so you could fix something for him, he would go to the tool box and come back confused, embarrassed and angry ... because he couldn't remember what a screwdriver was or what it looked like. Such is the invasive and cruel nature of Alzheimer's.)

But Dad, at our insistence, began a 15th volume. (His last complete book, "This I Remember ... Growing Up in Schenectady" was published in 1994.) He had certain conditions, however: he wanted to do the work on a typewriter -- the way he had done many of his early books and the way in which he had done many thousands of newspaper articles for *The Daily Gazette* (and *Schenectady Union-Star* before that) prior to the age of the

207

computer. Dad agreed to start a new, untitled book -- which would basically include some second looks at memories of his popular "Tales of Old Dorp" column in the *Gazette*. He agreed ... as long as he could complete his writing on a typewriter. My brother-in-law, Archie Munro, then planned to transcribe Dad's manuscript into a computer and put the work on a disk to send it to the publisher.

Truthfully, I had totally forgotten about the enterprise in recent years and assumed not much -- if anything -- had been written, because Dad's illness began to progress at a rapid rate. (My perception of what happened is that Dad got discouraged after awhile and just gave up the enterprise he had started. He realized he was having trouble spelling and coming out with 'Unien Streat' instead of 'Union Street;' things like that.)

Dad's long, sad battle with Alzheimer's came to a conclusion on February 10th, when another dreaded illness named Pneumonia also entered the picture and took my father quickly -- much in the same way that former President Ronald Reagan died in June of 2004.

Now, when Bonnie showed me the manuscript, though I recognized what it was right away, like Bonnie I was unsure of what, if anything, ought to be done with it. I just put it aside for a few days; I wanted to show it to my mother, Ruth Hart, and see what her feelings were about the lost, forgotten manuscript. But above all, I wanted to wait until the funeral was over to even talk about it with Mom and Bonnie, and I wanted even more time to pass before we actually did anything with it.

Ultimately, the decision was up to Mom. Should we publish the work at all, or should we just keep it in the family as an heirloom? Should we offer it to the *Gazette* and let them print it if they wanted to? If we do publish it, what would be the best format?

Finally, Mom asked me to decide. She said, "Give it some more thought; try to think what Dad would want us to do."

I DID give it a lot of thought ... and prayer. After a few months, I told Mom we ought to meet with Mr. Robert Kosineski

Sr., the skilled and kindly man who had published so many of Dad's earlier volumes at Benchemark Printing in Schenectady, and the same person who had done such a thorough and professional job of producing my own biography of my father, "Larry Hart, My Dad," in 2003.

It was "Bob K's" advice to us to combine this unfinished, unpublished but precious manuscript with my own current venture "Dear Old Scotia" and put my work and his work between the same book covers as one, single volume.

So ... here it is! From my own perspective, it is a great honor and thrill for me to have Dad's last work published together with my book about growing up in Scotia in the 1950s and 1960s. Am I sure it is what Dad would have wanted? I don't know; I can't answer that. But I know that Dad, who is in a better place now, somewhere out there is very happy that we have brought his last manuscript -- which he meant for you many faithful readers of his -- to you, at last, in some form.

Mom and Bonnie and I decided to illustrate his work with pictures connected to people and places mentioned in this manuscript, plus some selected photos from his colorful career as a reporter, columnist, historian, photographer and public speaker. It goes without saying, I suppose, but we in the family -- and that includes brothers, sister-in-laws, grandchildren and great-grandchildren ... everyone -- are extremely proud of my father. Did you know, for example, that Dad took official journalistic photos of five presidents? He did ... Harry Truman, Dwight Eisenhower, John Kennedy, Richard Nixon and Ronald Reagan, although Kennedy (senator), Nixon (vice-president) and Reagan (actor) were not presidents at the time Dad took their respective photos.

Well, enough of that. I'm through talking. This is Dad's turn -- his unpublished manuscript awaits you in the pages to come. I hope you enjoy it. I have a pretty good idea that you will!

ARH

A REMEMBRANCE OF MY "TALES OF OLD DORP"

By Larry Hart

I'll never forget February, 1974, when the *Schenectady Gazette* began printing my first columns of "Tales of Old Dorp."

What were my favorite tales? That's not easy to answer, because I enjoyed telling stories about Schenectady ... its people, parks, General Electric, ALCO, the Erie Canal, schools, bridges, etc.

Let's recall some of those memories; remembrances of the turn of the last century:

In the early 1900s, a Friday night might well have been called Faker's Night. This was the late afternoon when the main force of workers finished their long day's stint at GE or ALCO when the patent medicine men, snake oil peddlers and pitch men would station themselves at the foot of Crescent Park. But the Wasson (Park) House stable yard opening upon State Street at Barrett Street was a favorite stand for the fast-buck boys. They might work on a wagon or a hastily built platform. Kerosene oil or other torches lighted the scene.

To attract attention, the pitchmen used such props as an Indian with full headgear who did a dance to the accompaniment of his own whoops, a banjo player or simply a snare drummer who beat a quick-step tempo. The crowd grew as accomplices in the audience primed the pump by being first to buy a potato peeler or liniment that was practically a cure-all. They called them "Shills," a word coming from tent carnival use of the "shell game."

Larry Hart's colorful and hectic but happy career as a news photographer, reporter and columnist, historian and public speaker kept him busy throughout his adult life. In the top photo, Hart checks over a paragraph at the typewriter in his library at home in 1984. In the bottom right photo, he has some words to say to a gathering in the yard behind his beloved Schenectady County Historical Society on Nov. 14, 1976. The photo at bottom left is from December of 1997.

211

The Wasson House veranda was almost level with the sidewalk at the corner of State and Barrett Streets. Eillie Schedtel, later a restaurant waiter for many years, made and sold waffles at night, competing with the pitchmen. His batter cakes were a cent apiece with all the powdered sugar you could shake on.

* * *

There was a particular fascination to the old City Hall for young lads of Schenectady when the city jail was located in the basement of that old brick structure. This was the City Hall built in 1880 at Franklin and Jay Streets which was razed in 1929 to make way for the present City Hall that now occupies the entire block.

The jail floor was several feet below ground level on the Franklin Street side of the building. At the end toward Clinton Street (then White Street), a barred window permitted persons from outside to look into the cell space. When the window was open, it also allowed anyone inside there to talk with outsiders. A jailed man's head and shoulders would be in view. The prisoners often would talk to the youngsters, sometimes to the boys to buy cigarettes for them (usually "Sweet Caporals") but often to tell them of the evils of drink that caused human beings to end up in a barred cage. It was a lesson that could not be taught anywhere else. Girls never went near the place.

* * *

Way back into the olden days around 1850, there were only a few houses on State Street above the railroad which was the Utica-Schenectady road at that time.

The William Van Vranken property at the corner of State and Clinton Streets (now Bank of America) was then a boarding house known as the American House. The field between Clinton and Lafayette Streets was a favorite exhibition place for circuses and traveling horse shows. On the next block below was formerly a

When President Dwight D. Eisenhower stopped at the Schenectady railroad station on Oct. 23, 1952, Larry Hart (then a photographer for the old Schenectady Union-Star) was one of the journalists on hand for the occasion which drew thousands of interested spectators. Hart is visible in photo at the bottom right (his left elbow is right next to the bunting by the podium at Eisenhower's left) as he gets in position (page 214) to take the accompanying photographs looking upwards at "Ike." (Larry Hart collection.)

large pond and Sitterly's saw and grist mill. Occupying all the land fronting Broadway (then called Centre Street) between Smith and State Streets was the Pilling iron foundry.

Crescent Park (now Veterans Park) was the gift of Col. Robert C. Furman, who lived in the house that is now the rectory of St. Joseph's Church. About 1850, when Colonel Furman bought the property at the corner of Smith and Lafayette together with most of the land in that block, people thought he was being peculiar -- buying land so far outside the city. He had the house built about 1857. Not far from the Furman house was a large pond on which he kept a rowboat, and nearby a sparkling spring gushed from the roots of an old elm tree of centuries of growth. The spring was filled in about 1890.

* * *

Long, long ago, Schenectady always had an ability to present the same appearance year in and year out to those who visited here for any reason. It soon was said by outsiders to be "The only finished city in which the last nail had been driven and to which the last "finis" had been written; the only town with a fence around it and a ceiling overhead."

Schenectady was known as Old Dorp during the best part of the 19th century. It was the butt of jokers and wags from one end of the city to the other. However, the 1880s brought the change in Schenectady, and the middle of that decade marked the beginning of the present epoch in the city's history -- when it passed from the category of a horse and buggy town into an industrial center!

Dorp, a nickname which adhered to Schenectady, is simply an old Dutch word meaning village or settlement. It was originally, of course, an appropriate phrase since it was mainly the Dutch who settled here and pioneered the town's development. But during the 19th Century and up to 1886, it was used derisively -- usually intended as a slur on the city.

For many decades, the city had seemed to stand still. Whereas other cities of the country either progressed or died,

Larry Hart (first row, center), political reporter and columnist for the Schenectady Gazette, takes notes as he listens to Senator Robert F. Kennedy (foreground) during Kennedy's speech at City Hall in Schenectady on March 1, 1965. Frank Duci, Hart's longtime friend and former Mayor of Schenectady, is at Hart's left. In the bottom photo, Schenectady's finest news photographers of the time assemble for a photograph on April 3, 1956. In the front row, from left, are: Sidney Brown (Gazette), Evan Richards (Union-Star) and Ronald Rogers (Gazette.) In the back row, from left, are: Charles Sellers (Gazette), Larry Hart (Union-Star) and Edward Schultz (Union-Star.) (Larry Hart collection.)

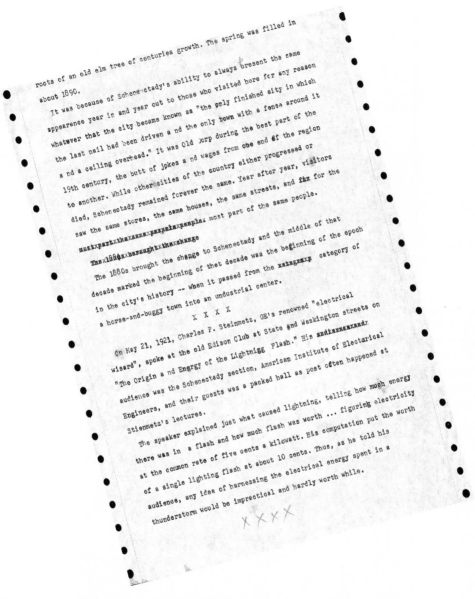

roots of an old elm tree of centuries growth. The spring was filled in about 1890.

It was because of Schenectady's ability to always present the same appearance year in and year out to those who visited here for any reason whatever that the city became known as "the only finished city in which the last nail had been driven and the only town with a fence around it and a ceiling overhead." It was Old Dorp during the best part of the 19th century, the butt of jokes and wages from one end of the region to another. While other cities of the country either progressed or died, Schenectady remained forever the same. Year after year, visitors saw the same stores, the same houses, the same streets, and far for the most part of the same people.

meet part xinxxxxxxxxxxxxxxx

The x1880sxbrought xthexchange
The 1880s brought the change to Schenectady and the middle of that decade marked the beginning of thet decade was the beginning of the epoch in the city's history -- when it passed from the xxxxxxxx category of a horse-and-buggy town into an undustrial center.

X X X X

On May 21, 1921, Charles P. Steinmetz, GE's renowned "electrical wizard", spoke at the old Edison Club at State and Weskington streets on "The Origin and Engrgy of the Lightnigg Flash." His xxxxxxxxxxxx audience was the Schenectady section, American Institute of Electarical Engineers, and their guests was a packed hall as post often happened at Stienmetz's lectures.

The speaker explained just what caused lightning, telling how much energy there was in a flash and how much flash was worth ... figuring electricity at the common rate of five cents a kilowatt. His computation put the worth of a single lighting flash at about 10 cents. Thus, as he told his audience, any idea of harnessing the electrical energy spent in a thunderstorm would be impractical and hardly worth while.

X X X X

Larry Hart went back to the comfort of his old typewriter, forsaking the computer, to write this, his last manuscript of what was to be his 15th book on Schenectady and area history. Here is a portion of the actual typed text.

217

Schenectady seemed to forever remain the same. Year after year, visitors saw the same stores, the same houses, the same streets and, for the most part, the same people! Nothing new came in the way of industries and very few new buildings were added to its quota. Even with the coming of the Erie Canal and the railroads, Schenectady was called "a sleepy little Dutch town; an Old Dorp if there ever was one." Some wags even said Schenectady had grown as much as it was ever going to grow.

But that all changed with the advent of the Edison Machine Works in 1886 and its magnificent growth into the General Electric Company before the turn of the century. The industrial expansion and population explosion made it "The City That Lights and Hauls the World" almost overnight.

Instead of Old Dorp, people began referring to Schenectady as the Electric City -- this time in awe of its reputation as an industrial center. However, we do occasionally still hear some old-timers refer to the community as Old Dorp -- in an affectionate manner, of course!

It was back in 1845 when the first supply of coal was delivered in Schenectady. Henry Ross, Schenectady's dealer in lumber with offices and yards on Dock Street (which became Erie Boulevard) and had the first delivery of coal brought here from Troy by wagon. The unloading of the black stones attracted a curious crowd. Some skeptics purchased small quantities of the new stuff and tried it on their woodburning stoves at home, but it wouldn't burn because the grates were not adapted for its use. Disgusted, these people then used the coal to fill in low spots in their gardens and driveways. Not long after, however, the burning of coal for stoves and furnaces became commonplace.

* * *

On May 21, 1921, Charles P. Steinmetz, GE's reknowned "Electrical Wizard," spoke at the old Edison Club on State and Washington Streets on "The Origin and Energy of the Lightning

Here's an early view of the General Electric Company grounds before 1910 ,,, probably during the 1890s. (Larry Hart collection.)

This is a shot of some boys taking lunches to their fathers at the GE ... probably around 1900. (Larry Hart collection.)

The main entrance of the GE plant, as it looked in 1917. (Larry Hart collection.)

Flash." His audience was the Schenectady Section of the American Institute of Electrical Engineers, and the lecture attracted a packed hall ... as often happened at Steinmetz's lectures.

The speaker explained just what caused lightning, telling how much energy there was in a flash and how much flash was worth ... figuring electricity at the common rate of five cents a kilowatt. His computation put the worth of a single lightning flash at about 10 cents. Thus, as he told his audience, any idea of harnessing the electrical energy spent in a thunderstorm would be impratical and hardly worthwhile.

* * *

Looking back at old publications can be eye-openers when they refer to one's hometown. Things we now take for granted -- such as parks, thickly settled residential areas and suburban living -- were once romanticized in local booklets printed by the Bureau of Trade or private industry.

I came across a pamphlet printed in 1915 by the Schenectady Railway Company that described in detail the wonders of public travel. There were so many places to go, even if it was only to enjoy the ride and a sight-seeing tour of a growing city and its environs.

There was this portion which had to do with seeing the "New Schenectady."

From the corner of the Union Station arcade and State Street, the traveler may turn to his left and facing the east, he many pass directly through the heart of Schenectady's business center. At the waiting room of the Schenectady Railway Company, he may board a car marked Union Avenue or else one labeled Rugy Road that will take him up the State Street hill with Crescent Park on his left and the new county courthouse building on his right. At the end of the park, the car turns to the left and passes the New York State Armory on the right. The car then turns into Nott Terrace, and in a few moments later the big

Engines at the American Locomotive Company, as they looked in this 1903 shot. (Larry Hart collection.)

223

twin-built high school of the city will be viewed on the left. At the corner of Union Street as the car turns to the east, the visitor must alight. He will find himself in front of the old blue gate entering Union College campus. Here he may certainly spend at least a pleasant hour viewing the handiwork of Dr. Eliphalet Nott and his successors of the last century and more.

At the trolley station, any streetcar bearing the label "G.E." would take the visitor to the largest electrical plant in the western hemisphere, if not the world ... the headquarters of the famous General Electric Company. From the waiting room at Lafayette and State Street, it was but a short walk westward along State Street to the corner of Jay Street. Turning there to the right and to the north, at the end of the first block would be found the three structures in which were housed the executives of the city's government. Another block further on would disclose the Federal Building and post office. This thoroughfare, if pursued a few blocks further, would also bring the tourist to the doors of the American Locomotive Company -- then one of the most widely famed concerns of its kind.

The most beautiful residential section of Schenectady, even at that time, could be partially viewed from the trolleys marked Union Avenue, Grand Boulevard, Rugby Road and Rosendale Road. Visible were the ornate but also comfortable and cozy homes of the people who have made Schenectady great.

A ride into the beautiful village of Scotia would not be overlooked by those who visited Schenectady. Streetcars marked Mohawk Avenue or Ballston Avenue would take them there. This trip would also include crossing the old bridge with a view of the venerable Mohawk River and a ride up the Scotia Dyke (Schenectady Avenue), which was erected over a century before for the purpose of taking the highway out of the marsh and placing it above a high water mark. Before entering the most settled part of the village, a short stop usually would be made at the ancient Glen Sanders Mansion -- a house filled with interest to those who delighted in relics of the past.

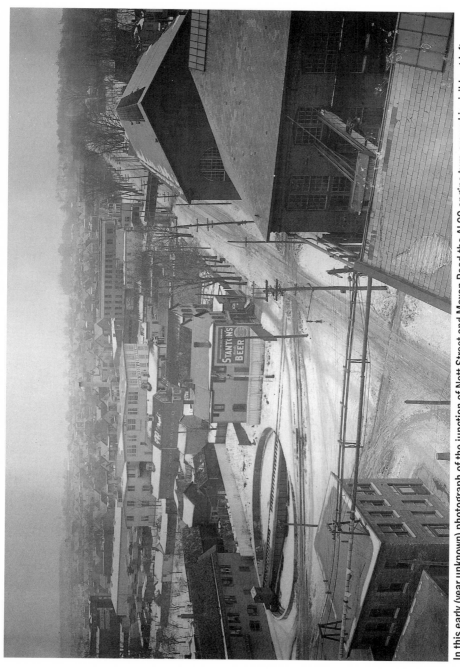

In this early (year unknown) photograph of the junction of Nott Street and Maxon Road the ALCO engine turn-around is visible at left. (Larry Hart collection.)

A crew of some of the men who worked at ALCO are shown in this photograph taken in 1890. (Larry Hart collection.)

* * *

There are few around Schenectady today who can recall the old Island Park, a sports area developed on what was once known as Van Slyck Island. But chances are that their memories of crossing the old pontoon bridge to reach it are scarce.

To a young lad or miss, it was a real treat to go to the island at the foot of State Street because it was an adventurous crossing on that bobbing floating span. Watching baseball games of the State League or Eastern League in those pre-World War I days was a family outing. Crossing the bridge was a childish anticipation both before and after the sports attraction. When it came time for the Van Curler Hotel about 1922, the Binnekill was relocated to a new channel nearer the island. The Edison Club was a few hundred feet downstream. It was all Frog Alley territory -- generally considered that sector south of State Street between the old Erie Canal and Washington Avenue.

What we know today as Hamilton Hill -- that section of higher land above Veeder Avenue and extending east to Brandywine Avenue -- was called by various names throughout the city's history. We are not certain where the name Bowery Hill or Bowery Woods was applied to the summit that overlooks the older portion of the city, but undoubtedly it came quite early after the settlement of Old Dorp. It is known that at least by 1800, inhabitants referred to it as the Bowery Hill or Bowery Woods. It probably got its name from its green cover of trees, principally lofty pitch pine but interspersed with elm and maple. The hill was sandy, with a deep underlay of clay partly exposed on a high space along lower Veeder Avenue. For many years, Bowery Woods was a favorite place for strollers and picnickers, because it was well-shaded and afforded a magnificent view of the river valley to the west.

The Alonzo C. Paige family owned the greater part of the hill area and eventually, as streets began to be developed (and trees taken down), that section became known as Paige Hill long before the turn of the century. These were the days when the Fair Grounds attracted large crowds to such events as circuses, agricultural exhibitions and horse races in the area now bounded roughly by Schenectady Street, Duane Avenue, Craig Street and Stanley Street.

The Fair Grounds ceased functioning after 1899 and was sold for housing lots in a public auction held by the city in 1901.

The hill section became known as Hamilton Hill once Hamilton Street extended through a portion of the old Fair Grounds. In the Schenectady building boom after 1900 came much of the home construction in upper Summit Avenue, Germania Avenue, Mulford Street, upper Paige Street and upper Schenectady Street. Between 1910 and 1919, the upper section of the old Fair Grounds was developed mainly by the Union Realty Co., headed by Samuel Dickhoff. His firm built most of the houses on the south side of Emmet and Craig to Steuben, Stanley Street, Lincoln Avenue and the north side of Duane Avenue. Summit Avenue marked the north boundary of the hill. Hamilton Street Hill provided the only cross-connection to downtown. On any given wintry day, handsleds and bobsleds coasting from a crest on an iced run on the hill ran as far as Center Street, now known as Broadway.

Way back in the olden days around 1850, there were only a few houses on State Street above the railroad which was the Utica-Schenectady road at that time. Crescent Park, now Veterans Park, between Smith and State, was the gift of Col. Robert G. Furman, Platt Potter and a few others who owned land along that portion of State Street.

* * *

On Jan. 3, 1930, it was announced in newspapers that large-sized paper money was soon to disappear, leaving only the smaller bills in circulation. The U.S. Treasury Department said the retirement of the large-sized bills had been ordered as of January 2nd, and that the banks would be instrumental in recalling them. In another few years, those who had saved the larger bills showed them off as an oddity.

Crescent Park (now Veterans Park) in Schenectady has long been a place for city folk and visitors to sit and relax downtown. The top photograph, looking east from a spot approximately where the Bank of America is now located, shows the park as it looked in 1875 when the Civil War monument was dedicated. In the bottom photo, we see the park as it appeared in 1910. (Larry Hart collection.)

FOUNTAIN AND BAND STAND, CRESCENT PARK
SCHENECTADY, N. Y.

Here is Crescent Park, in a photo from the late 1940s, taken from the Albany Street side in front of the area about where the Schenectady County Courthouse stands. Visible across the street are, from left, the Breslaw furniture store, the old Colonel Isaac Yates residence, the former Dr. Charles G. McMullen private medical center, the Elks Club and the old Plaza Theater. (Larry Hart collection.)

* * *

There were plenty of news items in Schenectady in 1914:

On April 6 that year, an old hostelry known as the Freeman House was demolished to make way for the projected construction of a new bridge (although actual work on the first Western Gateway Bridge did not come until 1934.) The building was located at the foot of State Street at Washington Avenue at what would become the entrance to the new bridge.

At the time of its being razed, local officials acknowledged that there was no accurate information as to the age of Freeman House. It had been called Knickerbocker Hall in its earliest days. However, one look at the ancient timbers, bricks and old carpentry belied its age. I suspect it was erected at about the dawn of the 19th century, just after Schenectady had become a chartered city.

Also in April of 1914, the Knights of Columbus opened their new home on Union Street just above Jay -- a handsome, two-story brick building that is still standing and now used as a professional office building. Toward the end of April that year, work on the new Schenectady County Jail on Veeder Avenue was completed. On May 21, 1914, the city of Schenectady requested the Public Service Commission to approve a new trolley car passenger rate -- six tickets (or tokens) for 25 cents. However, the PSC refused it and the straight nickel-a-ride fare of the Schenectady Railway Co. was retained.

Back in 1914, motion picture houses were still quite scarce because the industry was yet in its formative stage and films were not plentiful. The public, however, had by this time shown increasing interest in the "flicks" and began to clamor for bigger and more comfortable theaters.

There was even a propensity for many theater owners and viewers alike to accept the showing of motion pictures on Sundays as perfectly moral and legal. However, until 1914 there was a controversy over that issue, and many theaters that showed movies on Sunday were closed down by local law. A court

The old City Hall on Franklin and Jay Streets is shown in this 1928 photograph. (Larry Hart collection.)

test in Binghamton resolved the issue when a Supreme Court decision handed down on Sept. 13, 1914, ruled that Sunday movies were not in violation of state law.

It was just about this time that Schenectady's newest movie theater -- the Lincoln Theater on Brandywine Avenue near Albany Street -- opened. It advertised admission prices at five cents and ten cents, and would open every afternoon and evening, including Sundays, showing from 1:30 p.m. to 10:30 p.m. Other movie houses at that time were the Happy Hour on Center Street, the Orpheum on State Street near the Broadway corner, the Crescent Theater on State Street opposite Jay Street, the Bijou Theater in the Odd Fellows Hall at Crane Street and Chrisler, and the Congress Theater at Congress and Third. The Van Curler Opera House at Franklin and Jay offered live stage performances then, but later also incorporated some movie shows into its schedule.

This was a decade before the construction of the spacious downtown theaters such as the State, Proctors and Wedgeway (which was the first Proctors.)

* * *

Let's go further back into Schenectady's history to things that were happening in March of 1880:

The Mohawk Gas Company was having trouble with its underground pipelines. Certain sections of the Third and Fourth Wards had no gaslight for several nights, so candles and kerosene lamps were utilized in private homes and in the Second Reformed and Methodist churches for services.

Citizens were complaining that the streets of Schenectady were filled with mud and should be cleaned.

William H. Peckham offered choice building lots for Summit Avenue and Mumford Street which he said he would sell at fair prices and on easy terms. Construction about town promised to have a brisk season. Henry S. DeForest had just purchased from

This is the way the area of Hamilton Street to Broadway (then known as Center Street) appeared to city dwellers around 1880. (Larry Hart collection.)

The interior of Union Station of the old Schenectady Railroad Station on Erie Boulevard holds memories for many older Schenectadians. In the top photo taken in 1962, we see the large, wooden benches that were always a welcome sight for weary travelers and those waiting for trains. In the center photo, train caller Edward J. Patten is on the job on Dec. 3, 1947. The familiar, large window with the clock in the center is visible in this shot taken in September of 1963. (Larry Hart collection.)

These outdoor shots of the train station show passengers (top photo) waiting for a train in 1947, while the bottom photo -- from a rainy day in 1948 -- reminds us of how the outside of the station appeared back then. (Larry Hart collection.)

Jonas H. Crane several lots in Center Street just south of the gas works that became the Ten Eyck Apartments on Broadway.

A Niskayuna correspondent for the *Evening Star* wrote that "Fishing in the Mohawk River was never better, if as good as present." He went on to write, "Crowds are visiting Niskayuna every few days from Albany, Troy and Schenectady bent on angling. Some very large messes have been caught. The continued high water has resulted in the accumulation of an immense number of fish, principally bass and pike, in the river. Owing to its being very secluded, Niskayuna is the best fishing grounds. Eugene Stowe, the station agent and owner of a large number of fishing boats, says that the season promises to be the best in years."

A driver in the employ of George Luckhurst, proprietor of the Myers House on Liberty Street just below the Erie Canal, drove into the hotel yard with a team of horses. Being cold, the driver stopped the team at the side entrance to the hotel and without hitching the horses, went inside to hotel to warm his hands. The horses started to walk down to the barn but must have been frightened, for they ran clear through the Myers Arcade and burst through the swinging doors at the State Street end and then turned to run down the street and demolished the entrance to Harry DeKeiter's barber shop. The runaways were finally caught at the lower end of the city.

William L. Sanders, a receiver for the Clute Brothers, announced there would be a public auction on March 29 of the old machine shop located between Liberty and Union Streets and between the railroad and canal. The Clute shop was where the turret mechanism for the famed U.S.S. Monitor was manufacured during the Civil War.

A pool tournament was held at Charles Wiencke's Hotel Germania at the northwest corner of Liberty and Center (now Broadway) Streets. The attendance was large and included many prominent business and professional men from Schenectady, Albany, Troy, Cohoes, Saratoga Springs, Ballston Spa and Amsterdam.

* * *

Here's a look at some of the things that were happening locally during January of 1921:

The eminent electrical engineers of General Electric Co. spoke at separate functions that month on the subject of electricity and the part it would play in America's future. Dr. Charles P. Steinmetz was in Baltimore where he declared the world "Has only begun to use electricity, and it is this force which will make housekeeping more and more easy in the future."

"There are new devices of every kind to make housework lighter, and their use will grow tremendously in the future," he declared. During World War I, the cost of nearly everything else went up, but the cost of electric current remained low. In the future, mines would be electrified and the cost of coal reduced, and with that would come a reduction in the cost of current. Electricity eased many house chores and problems of the American housewife during World War I.

The winter was mild in New York State in 1921. Therefore, the State College of Agriculture advised farmers and ice cutters to "take the first opportunity (to harvest ice) because you may not get another" to get the maximum thickness

Charles Steinmetz and Thomas A. Edision, two brilliant men whose names are etched in history for their inventions and electrical advances, sit side-by-side in what would be their last-ever meeting in March of 1922. Steinmetz and Edison are watching a demonstration of Steinmetz's lightning machine in the Building 28 laboratory at the GE. (Larry Hart collection.)

of good ice. The college said snow should not be allowed to lie on the ice surface, since it tends to prevent further thickening. In general, ice was not harvested in New York until at least eight inches thick, although the average thickness was 12 inches. The river and lake ice in January, 1921, was not even the minimum and it was guessed that it "may be necessary this year to harvest comparatively thin ice."

* * *

Let's move ahead to the 1930's:

Statistics given out by the Federal Emergency Relief Administration (FERA) invariably told the public what it already knew -- things were getting worse in the field of economics. In March, 1935, they announced that the number of New York State families increased from 465,993 in December to 472,780 in January, and the cost incident therefore advanced from $30.1 million to $30.2 million. However, it may have been encouraging to those of this state to know that the increase in the number of families being added was only half as great as the general average of the whole country.

By September of 1935, it was announced that the number of families and single resident persons on relief in Schenectady during August was five percent below the July figure. There were 3,130 cases of welfare recorded in July as compared to 2,963 in August. However, the cost of maintenance rose from $119,244 to $120,785. People in those days were on and off welfare, sometimes one month to the next, as family breadwinners found part-time or short-term employment enough to enable them to get off the rolls for a time. Men who were out of work during the Great Depression did odd jobs whenever possible and many women did extra baking, sewing or laundry work so that the family could scrape along on a few dollars a week. Some older people today reflect on those hectic days of the Depression Thirties and still are most proud of the fact that they never did go on the public rolls.

Union College's freshman class, the class of 1939, registered on Sept. 11 and numbered 225. The opening of Union's 140th year was Sept. 16 with the welcoming addresses by President Dixon Ryan Fox and Dr. Ernest M. Ligon, professor of psychology. Miss Frances Travis, in charge of the student employment bureau at the college, noted a change in the attitude of students toward various kinds of jobs during the Depression, with the result that students were willing to accept any kind of work. There was, however, a marked decrease in the number of jobs offered by local business firms because of the drop in regular employment.

That same week, record crowds of shoppers passed through the new supermarket on Broadway at Hamilton Street in quarters that had been modernized from the converted Wiederhold factory. It was under the personal direction management of Grosberg, president of Grosberg-Golub Co. The supermarket type of merchandising was a brand-new venture.

Wedekind Motors Inc. opened its new building, including garage, offices and showroom at 1595 State Street, with formal ceremonies conducted the morning of Sept. 14. Ernest C. Wedekind and his son, George Wedekind, were sales and service managers, respectively.

During September of 1935, two former heavyweights who were champions stopped in this area. The first was Jack Dempsey, whose party was forced to stop in Scotia the afternoon of Sept. 15 while a balky carburetor on his 16-cylinder sedan was repaired. He was on his way back from Speculator where they watched Max Baer train (at the old Osborne Inn on Lake Pleasant) for his upcoming fight with Joe Louis. Dempsey was in Scotia for about 20 minutes, but word soon got around that he was there -- with the result that he shook a lot of hands, signed many autograph books and posed for snapshots by both young and old amateur photographers.

The second was Max Baer himself, who motored down to

Schenectady on the afternoon of Sept. 24 to catch a train to New York City and his fight with Joe Louis at Yankee Stadium. Baer, looking tan and healthy, walked briskly around the block while waiting for the arrival of the North Shore Limited, leaving at 3:08 p.m. Hard on his heels was a gang of cheering youngsters. In about seven hours, Baer would be on the canvas, taking the count of 10 in the fourth round.

* * *

Rear Admiral Richard E. Byrd, serial conqueror of both the North and South Poles, lectured at Mont Pleasant High School auditorium on the afternoon of Oct. 3, 1935. His talk was augmented by 9,000 feet of motion pictures illustrating his expedition.

Also in 1935, this area had experienced a bitter winter, weatherwise, as subzero temperatures often prevailed for weeks at a time.

The presentation of an oil portrait of Dr. Charles P. Steinmetz, former professor of electrical enginerring at Union College, was one of the features of the ninth annual Steinmetz Memorial Lecture in the college's Memorial Chapel the night of March 14, 1935. Dr. Robert A. Doherty, dean of the Yale School of Engineering, delivered the principal address. Roy C. Muir, GE vice-president, formally presented the portrait, a work of Harold Mott-Smith, to President Dixon Ryan Fox.

The Schenectady Taxpayers Association, in a communication to local banks, suggested that banks reduce interest on real estate loans from six to five percent as an aid to property owners and economic recovery. It was pointed out in the communication that interest in bank deposits had been reduced from 4 1/2 percent to 2 1/2 percent, while there had been no general reduction in the interest charged by banks on mortgages.

The Boston Store, located at 121-129 Broadway, celebrated the 35th year of its establishment. It had become a business on

Old Nott Terrace High School, as it looked in 1952. (Larry Hart collection.)

March 19, 1900, under the guidance of Joseph E. Dwyer, as a small drygoods located adjacent to the old Ellis House -- a noted hostelry of that period, and later to be the site of the former Woolworth store. In 1906, a disastrous fire destroyed the store, and then it was located on the corner block of Smith Street and Broadway. Mr. Dwyer was still head of the Boston Store in 1935. Also celebrating an anniversary, its 19th, was Vinick's Men's Shop at 467 State Street, to where it had moved in 1932. Maurice and Louis Vinick were the founders and proprietors. Later, the store moved up for its long stay at 514 State Street at the corner of Lafayette.

In a village election on the day of March 18, John F. Sible, Republican, was elected mayor of Scotia. With him were elected: Harold Lewis, Republican, and Merle Kelefant, Republican, as trustees. Fred Colwell, another Republican, was elected police justice. One of the surprises of the election was the heavy vote polled on behalf of Lewis, a newcomer in village politics. He later was to become Glenville superintendent and chairman of the County Board of Supervisors.